POSITIVE SCHOOL DISCIPLINE
A practical guide to developing policy

The authors are indebted to the executors of the Annie V. Moore Estate for assistance with the publication of this book — a venture designed to contribute to the well being, guidance and development of children and youth in schools.

POSITIVE SCHOOL DISCIPLINE
A practical guide to developing policy

Revised Edition

Margaret Cowin, Liz Freeman, Alan Farmer,
Meryl James, Ailsa Drent and Ray Arthur
Illustrations by Esther Cullen

LONGMAN

First published, 1985, by Parents and Friends of Monnington Publications, 123 Bouverie St., Carlton, Victoria 3053, Australia.

Revised edition published 1990 by Narbethong Publications, P.O. Box 238, Boronia Vic 3155, Australia.

Copyright © Margaret Cowin, Liz Freeman, Alan Farmer, Meryl James, Ailsa Drent, Ray Arthur, 1990.

First published in Great Britain 1991 by
Longman Industry and Public Service Management,
Longman Group UK Limited, 6th Floor, Westgate House,
The High, Harlow, Essex CM20 1YR, England
Tel Harlow (0279) 442601
Fax Harlow (0279) 444501 Group 3 2
Reprinted July 1992

Not for sale in Australia, New Zealand and Canada.

British Library Cataloguing-in-Publication Data
Cowin, Margaret
Positive school discipline: A practical guide to developing policy.
I. Title
371.1

ISBN 0-582-08713-9

Other than for the purposes and subject to the conditions prescribed under the Copyright Act, except for the five discussion papers in Section 10, no part of this publication may in any form or by any means (electronic, mechanical, microcopying, recording or otherwise) be reproduced, stored in a retrieval system or transmitted without prior written permission.

Special note; Section 10 only.
The publishers grant to all teachers and schools and to all lecturers and tertiary institutions the right to copy, photocopy or quote the articles in Section 10 for the purpose of discussion provided that the source is acknowledged.

Produced by Longman Group (FE) Ltd
Printed by Antony Rowe Ltd, Chippenham, Wiltshire.

Contents

Foreword	IX
Introduction	XIII
Definitions	XV

Part One: The Process — 1
Outline of the Process — 3

Phase A: Decide whether or not to start — 5
Step 1: Find out if discipline is a hot topic in your school — 6
Step 2: Discover what a review of discipline could involve — 7
Step 3: Create interest — 8
Step 4: Decide whether or not to review your discipline policy — 9

Phase B: Plan — 11
Step 5: Determine who will organise the review — 12
Step 6: Determine how decisions are to be reached in the review — 13
Step 7: Plan how to proceed — 14
Step 8: Let everybody know and ask them to be involved — 15

Phase C: Find out what actually happens in your school — 17
Step 9: Gather any policy statements that have a bearing on discipline — 18
Step 10: Identify discipline practices used within your school — 19
Step 11: Get reaction of parents, teachers, students to present practices and policies — 20
Step 12: Find out people's expectations of school discipline — 21
Step 13: Produce and distribute a progress report — 22

Phase D: Prepare your discipline policy — 23
Step 14: Agree on the framework for your new policy — 24
Step 15: Decide on the aims of your policy — 25
Step 16: Explore a variety of ways of achieving your aims — 26
Step 17: Select acceptable options — 28
Step 18: Produce a draft policy — 29
Step 19: Distribute draft policy for approval — 30

Phase E: Put the policy into practice — 31
Step 20: Establish an implementation group — 32
Step 21: Identify and provide skill development for all groups — 33
Step 22: Launch and promote the policy — 34
Step 23: Monitor practice — 35

Part Two: Ways and Means — 37
Section 1: Getting people working together — 39
Team building — 40
Mediation group model — 40
Outside consultants — 41
Circulars — 42
Making a video — 42
Discussion starters — 43
Responding to resistance — 43
Community meetings — 45
Making official documents matter — 47

Section 2: Values clarification — 49
What do we mean by discipline? — 51
What is important to me? — 51
Describing school behaviour — 53
Voting with your feet — 55
Memories of school — 57

Section 3: Surveys, observations and interviews — 59
Written surveys — 60
Sample survey questions: — 62
    School and classroom discipline — 62
    Analysis of school climate and organisation — 64
    Clarifying roles and responsibilities — 67
Observations — 68
Sample observation forms — 70
Interviews — 74
Inter-school visits — 74
Gathering information from students — 75

Section 4: Meetings and group discussions — 77
Group discussions — 78
Classroom meetings — 78

Brainstorming	81
Force-field analysis	82
Nominal group technique	85
Policy improvement planning sheet	86
Modified community conference technique	89

Section 5: In-service education 91
Guest speakers 93
Films and videos 93
Making workshops work 93
Sample agenda for workshop: Improving our policy 95
In-service or community meeting planning sheet 95
Sample programme for primary school in-service 98
Sample programme for a post-primary in-service 100

Section 6: Working out differences through discussion 103
The No-lose Method of conflict resolution 105
Glasser's eight steps of Reality Therapy for the classroom teacher ... 108
Contracting as part of the problem-solving process 109

Section 7: Planning an approach to confrontations 111
'You can't make me': teacher–student confrontations 112
Prevention is better than cure 113

Section 8: Aspects of positive policies and practices 115
Do well disciplined schools have anything in common? 116
Eight goals for developing a well disciplined school 116
Critical areas in the development of positive behavioural
   management strategies 119
What would a co-ordinated student welfare and discipline system look like? ... 120
Chandler High School welfare and discipline policy 121

Section 9: Rules and consequences 125
A three-stage approach 126
Consequences 129
Workshop: Developing consequences 130
Sample rules from schools:
   Yarrunga Primary School 131
   South Street, Moe, Primary School 131
   Maryborough Primary School 134

Section 10: Discussion papers — 137
Student behaviour: What can psychology tell us? Liz Freeman — 137
Is discipline a curriculum issue? Margaret Cowin — 141
Corporal punishment. Margaret Cowin — 147
Self-esteem: What is it? How can we enhance it? Ailsa Drent — 149
Social skills: Can we teach students to behave? Liz Freeman — 151

Part Three: References and Resources — 155
References — 157
Resources (under topic headings) — 159
Reports and general issues relating to discipline — 160
Leadership and the process of change in schools — 161
Evaluation — 163
Group participation in decision making — 163
Parent and community participation — 164
Student involvement and responsibility in school and community — 166
Staff development and in-service training — 167
Curriculum and teaching methods as preventive approaches to discipline — 168
School climate and organisation — 169
Student welfare — 172
Interpersonal skills (for teachers) — 172
Assertion training (for teachers) — 173
Self-esteem, social skills training and value clarification for students — 174
School rules — 176
Behaviour management:
    Resources covering a range of models — 176
    Assertive models — 177
    Behaviour modification — 177
    Cognitive behaviour modification and Rational Emotive Therapy — 179
    Reality Therapy — 179
    Dreikurs and Systematic Training for Effective Teaching — 181
    Thomas Gordon and Effectiveness Training — 182
    Transactional Analysis — 183

Additional Resources for the Revised Edition — 183
Books — 183
Annotated Bibliographies — 187
Short Articles — 187
Videos — 191

Foreword

For the greater part of this century school discipline has required a system of strong teacher control with a corresponding student compliance — an arrangement generally endorsed by society.

However, increasingly, school discipline has become a focus of community debate with many people challenging current practices as being outmoded, ineffective, inappropriate or inhumane.

A number of factors has contributed to this. These include:
- a more general awareness of how children develop and the need to apply this to curriculum practices;
- increased knowledge about effective learning strategies;
- changing relationship models in society leading to a belief that those between student/teacher/parents should be mutually supportive;
- the idea that each of these parties has rights which must be taken into account;
- a recognition that the school has a critical role to play in developing students increasing responsibility for their own behaviours;
- concern about the limitations and hazards of discipline systems either based largely on punishment or on the pendulum swing where adults have backed off from disciplining young people at all;
- increasing retention of young people at school, who, in the past, would have had considerable responsibility and power in the wider community;
- the argument that many students are not motivated to learn.

Reflecting the local and international level of interest in the subject, the Education Department of Victoria set up a Working Party in 1983 to consider the abolition of corporal punishment in schools and suggest alternative approaches.

As well as collating information and writing material for the working party, the authors, who were all members of Counselling, Guidance and Clinical Services staff at the time, became widely involved in assisting school communities to develop discipline policies.

Although each of the authors has moved into different spheres of education since, our interest and involvement in the area of school discipline has remained and been deepened through our changed perspectives.

We have been continually reminded that it is an on-going issue for schools both in this country and abroad. As we have continued to work with school communities we have become even more aware that:
- arriving at total school discipline policies and practices is a very complex process; it is also a time consuming one;
- teachers are increasingly being asked to take responsibility for the teaching of an even wider range of behaviours and skills (including that of developing self-discipline in students), than ever before;
- teachers are entitled to community understanding and support as they attempt these tasks;
- it is essential for parents to be involved. This is necessary so that they can convey the kinds of behavioural expectations they value — of great significance where groups within our multi-cultural society have different ideas. It also provides the opportunity to establish a link between home and school behaviour. Note that this does not imply that young people always behave in the same way at home as at school — for example, in the freedom they have to move around. What it does mean is that parents understand and support the expectation of the behaviour of the students at school, while the teachers recognise the values subscribed to at home. Further, involvement of parents allows them to support the teachers in developing responsible behaviour in students so that teaching and learning can take place.
- the critical link between the curriculum being offered by a school and the impact this can have on discipline is being increasingly recognised.
- recent studies into the sources of teacher stress have highlighted the importance of addressing matters of student discipline.

We are also pleased to note that there is an increasing range of resource materials available for schools to use in the development of positive discipline policies. We have included an additional list later in the book.

This book represents the collective knowledge and experience accumulated by the authors who readily acknowledge their indebtedness to the wider educational community.

Although all six authors worked on the conceptualisation and writing, individuals made specific contributions. Alan Farmer was responsible for funding and encouraging the group to tackle the

task. Margaret Cowin co-ordinated the project and Meryl James was responsible for the reference section. Liz Freeman contributed a wealth of ideas and materials developed in conjunction with Dandenong Student Services Centre, notably:
discussion starters, policy improvement planning sheet, sample workshops; improving our policy, and developing consequences, and sample primary and secondary school I.S.E. programmes.

In addition our thanks go to Peter Ruzyla who contributed the article *Critical areas in the development of positive behavioural management strategies* and to Chandler High School, Chelsea Heights, Yarrunga, Maryborough and South St, Moe, primary schools for permission to use their materials. *Classroom meetings* was adapted from P. McCarthy's article in *InterView* No. 10, 1983, and the *No-lose Method of conflict resolution* from *Reality Therapy and Education* "I'd like to see you after class, Jo" by L. Freeman, G. Hont and P. McCarthy in *InterView* No. 8, 1982.

We are also indebted to individual members of the Education Department for their ready informal sharing of professional knowledge about writing and publishing, and to our initial publishers, the Parents and Friends of Monnington, for their assistance.

Finally we recognise the contributions made by other Student Services staff, in particular, Bernard Barber (Reading Treatment and Research Centre), Martin Grigg (Shepparton Student Services, C. G. and C. S.), Ray Wilks (Coburg Student Services C. G. and C. S.) and office support staff Val Magree, Lisa Moyes, Areti Kourtis, Jan McNaughton, Irene Baldwin, Beth Platt, Josie Librizzi, Jane Lithoxopoulous and Kerry Dalliston.

Remaining convinced that the process of developing sound discipline policies and practices as outlined in this book can assist schools and their communities, we are pleased to offer this revised edition.

Introduction

We are convinced that enormous benefits result when a school community goes through the proper processes of developing a discipline policy of its own. This conviction about the value of the process itself is based on our work with schools that have successfully undertaken the task.

Our experience in such schools has shown that you can expect to achieve a relaxed atmosphere in which people spend more time on teaching and learning and less on managing difficult behaviour. These schools focus on identifying problems and solving them in advance, rather than dealing with them after they occur.

Where members of a school community have worked together to develop their policy, we have observed that parents, teachers and students have a much better understanding of the school rules; parents have confidence that the school has a positive sense of direction; teachers know they have the consistent backing of other staff in handling students; there is more co-operation among the students themselves and a greater sense of responsibility.

We believe these improvements have not happened by chance. Instead, they are the result of careful planning and action.

The successful schools seem to have ensured, firstly, that everybody who was going to be affected by a decision had a chance to have a say in it from the beginning, and that there were clear ways in which any member of the school community could contribute to the process. Secondly, care was taken to collect a great deal of information, on existing practices and theoretical alternatives, for example, as a basis for decisions. Thirdly, the process of developing a policy was not rushed through; at each step, checks were made to ensure that people had time to think about and react to any proposal.

We wrestled with the best way to share our experiences. In the end, we decided to describe the process of developing a discipline policy as though a school were starting from scratch.

Although we have confined ourselves to discussing the development of a 'discipline' policy, we recognise that this must be done in the context of broader policy statements about school aims and curriculum proposals. We also appreciate that discipline is part of all the provisions made by a school to ensure the well being of students and teachers.

We begin by talking about what 'you' might do, 'you' being a single reader. And indeed, that is where some most creative things have started, with a single person in a school. Although one person may get the idea off the ground, it cannot (must not) be continued by a one man band. Others need to be involved. The reader will become aware from the context, where the 'you' no longer refers simply to the reader, but to the group which is necessarily gathered together for the task.

In real life of course, our description has some artificiality. Some members of staff may have already worked on some elements of a discipline policy, others may have had no involvement. A beginning may have been made on a total policy and then teachers transferred, students came and went or the principal retired.

Nevertheless, we believe that all steps of the process need to be attended to by the school community if the end result is to be effective. (We have observed problems, for example, when, in an effort to be economical in terms of time, a small group has developed the policy and presented it for agreement. In by-passing the initial phases of awareness raising and information collection the sense of ownership of the policy is greatly diminished.) The co-ordinators of the review must be aware of changes in the community and ensure new members are brought up to date on what has happened and how contributions can be made.

We have described the process in a 'step one' 'step two' fashion in order to be as clear as possible. This will not necessarily be how it happens in practice. For example, a school may already have set up a co-ordinating group (Phase B) before going through the steps of Phase A; or a crisis may mean some later step has to be tackled urgently. Nevertheless, each of the steps identified contributes to the total result and we urge you to consider them all carefully.

Working through the total process will take some time — a year at least, schools tell us — but the benefit should be worth it.

We have suggested that the development of a school policy (if you have to start from the very beginning) is a five-phase process, with each phase containing a number of steps.

Part One of this book, The Process, discusses the five phases and details the contributing steps.

In Part Two: Ways and Means, you will find practical hints on how to develop the policy.

Part Three: References and Resources provides a list of books, videos and films, arranged under topic headings to help you select appropriate resources.

We wish you good reading and good practice.

Outline of the Process of Developing a Discipline Policy

Phase A Decide whether or not to start	Phase B Plan	Phase C Find out what actually happens in your school	Phase D Prepare your discipline policy	Phase E Put the policy into practice
Steps: 1. Find out if discipline is a hot topic in your school. 2. Discover what a review of discipline could involve. 3. Create interest. 4. Decide whether or not to review your discipline policy.	**Steps:** 5. Determine who will organise the review. 6. Determine how decisions are to be reached in the review. 7. Plan how to proceed. 8. Let everyone know and ask them to be involved.	**Steps:** 9. Gather any policy statements that have a bearing on discipline. 10. Identify discipline practices used within your school. 11. Get reaction of parents, teachers, students to present practices and policies. 12. Find out people's expectations of school discipline. 13. Produce and distribute a progress report.	**Steps:** 14. Agree on the framework for your new policy. 15. Decide on the aims of your policy. 16. Explore a variety of ways of achieving your aims. 17. Select acceptable options. 18. Produce a draft policy. 19. Distribute a draft policy for approval.	**Steps:** 20. Establish an implementation group. 21. Identify and provide skill development for all groups. 22. Launch and promote the policy. 23. Monitor practice.
Outcome: A decision will have been made on an informed basis by members of the school community on whether or not to review the school discipline policy at the moment. Those who will be involved have indicated their support.	**Outcome:** A plan will have to be made about: • how the policy development will proceed; • who will be involved and how; • who will be responsible; • a timeline.	**Outcome:** Information will have been gathered about existing policies, practices and attitudes towards discipline in your school. A summary/report of this will have been produced.	**Outcome:** A draft policy stating aims and objectives and detailing how these are to be achieved will have been written and distributed for approval.	**Outcome:** A policy has been accepted and is in practice, having been trialled, modified if necessary, and agreed to by all sections of the school community.

Positive School Discipline: A practical guide to developing policy   3

Definitions

Discipline:
Instruction having for its aim to form the pupil to proper conduct and action . . . A system or method for the maintenance of order, a system of rules for conduct . . . Correction.
— **The Oxford English Dictionary**, Clarendon Press, Oxford, 1933

Positive School Discipline:
This concept has several essential elements, namely:
- an agreed system of curriculum delivery which aims to create an harmonious learning environment;
- a code of behaviour which is known and accepted;
- consistent implementation of this at all levels;
- acknowledgement of those who keep the spirit of the code;
- deliberate teaching to develop self-discipline and responsibility;
- correction of behaviour that is outside the code.

Policy:
A policy is a set of principles which guide action.

School Policy:
- sets out the general goals of the school;
- outlines how the school expects to achieve those goals;
- provides a framework within which action can be taken in a consistent way; and
- lets the school community know what is aimed for and what can be expected of the school.

— **Curriculum Policy Making: An Introduction for School Councils**, Education Department of Victoria, 1984.

A Positive School Discipline Policy:
Is one aspect of a total school policy. It is an expression of the aims of the school community for the behaviour of its members towards each other so that they can work productively together. It describes how the school plans to teach students how to behave responsibly, co-operatively and with concern towards others and how they will be given opportunities to practise these behaviours.

It outlines how the school and teaching can be organised so that most problems are prevented and those that occur are dealt with constructively. The emphasis is on positive action rather than punishment.

Part One:

The Process

Phase A

Decide whether or not to start

A review of school discipline can have many benefits for your school. For example, it can lead to:
- greater involvement by teachers, parents, and students;
- a better understanding by all parties of why a school does things, for example, has a uniform;
- a focus on shared problem solving rather than witch-hunting;
- a positive, preventive approach to discipline.

School resources are limited. However, you will need to decide if discipline is an important and urgent issue.

To make such a decision you should follow these steps:
1. Find out if discipline is a hot topic in your school.
2. Discover what a review of a discipline could involve.
3. Create interest.
4. Decide whether or not to review your discipline policy.

The outcome of going through these steps should be:
- A decision will have been made on an informed basis by members of the school community on whether or not to review the school discipline policy at the moment. Those who will be involved have indicated their support.

Step 1: Find out if discipline is a hot topic in your school

Great things have small beginnings. Somebody has to start the process. Who should do this? How could it be done?

It could be that the principal, the vice-principal or someone deputised by them decides to find out informally if members of the school community are interested or concerned or confused about discipline in the school. One way to do this might be:
- to ask each individual parent, teacher, member of ancillary staff or student met during a week the following question, "What is your impression of discipline in this school?'
- to ask further questions only if the first answer needs clarifying, for example, 'What do you mean by that?' or 'Can you give me an example?'
- to limit the time spent with each person by saying, 'Thank you for those ideas. I hope we will be able to discuss them further later.'
- to collect data by jotting down notes, for example:
  Student A: 'teachers have pets'.
  Student B: 'most teachers are fair'.
  Parent C: likes having the school rules.
  Parent D: doesn't think teachers are strict enough.

Or it might be a teacher who starts the ball rolling by recording a class discussion or asking students to write about how school could be better.

Or it could be a parent member of the school council who raises the discipline issue at a meeting and asks the staff representative or the principal to discuss it with the staff.

Little questions can have big results, for example:
- 'Should the school have a uniform?'
- 'How long can students be kept in?'
- 'When are the rolls marked?'

Or it could be a student or group of students, particularly if the school has an organisation like a students representative council, who could ask questions of the principal or school council, for example:
- 'What can be done about crowding at lockers?'
- 'What can we do about kids who disrupt our classes?'
- 'What do we do about the teacher who always turns up late?'

Comments:

Beginners can find it hard to really listen and understand what people say in answer to a question. It is all too easy to make other people's answers fit into one's own ideas. A useful strategy to check that you have the other's meaning clear is to rephrase the answer with a question. 'Do you mean...?'

(Other ideas that could be used to find out views on existing school discipline are in Part Two: Ways and Means, in the sections listed below.)

What if:
- Some groups within the school feel that discipline is a real concern and others don't?
- Only one group feels there is concern?
- Only the principal thinks it would be a good idea to address the discipline policy issue now?

If any, or even all, of these apply see Step 3: Create interest, and 'Responding to resistance' in Ways and Means, Section 1.

See Part Two: Ways and Means—

Section 1: Getting people working together
- Discussion starters
- Responding to resistance

Section 3: Surveys, observations and interviews
- All articles

Section 4: Meetings and group discussions
- All articles

Step 3: Create interest

Others may not be as aware as you are that there are benefits in reviewing the discipline policy. You may have to help them see the light. List the formal groups in the school with the power to influence decisions, for example:
- co-ordinators
- school council
- parent club
- students representative council
- administrators

You will need to gain the interest of each group in the idea of reviewing the discipline policy.

Write down why you think the discipline policy needs reviewing and some advantages of doing this.

Using these ideas, you could then:
- Send the different groups a brief paper outlining the main points;
- Ask for a short time to speak about them at a meeting;
- Give a member of a group your notes and ask that they be presented;
- Write a letter, so that it has to be recorded in the minutes.

Other alternatives are:
- Send the groups the result of a small survey or class discussion and ask them to discuss it.
- Use a newspaper cutting to ask a question like, 'What can we do about this?', 'Do you think we should find out if this is happening at our school?'
- Ask a representative group of the school community to visit another school with an interesting programme.
- Ask a member of the school community to read official documents or review an article or a book on the topic and report back to a general meeting.
- Talk about your interest and concern informally.
- Pin up newspaper cuttings or articles on noticeboards in different places around the school. Cartoons can be especially attention attracting.
- Leave relevant items in the staffroom where they can be glanced at during lunchtime and other breaks.
- Ask the librarian to prepare a display - reading list, perhaps in conjunction with another member of staff.
- Invite a guest speaker (see Part Two: Ways and Means, Section 5).
- Show a film or a video (see Part Three: References and Resources for suggestions).

Next, think about the people in your school community who you know influence decisions. Keep your eyes and ears open for people who can put a point of view across and get agreement from others. Be alert for this in the classroom, staffroom or meetings and make sure you give these people the necessary information.

There are some people, however, who express their ideas so strongly, so loudly, so threateningly, or so inflexibly that others stay silent rather than trying to match this display. If you can't get such might on your side, at least make sure that you can count on the support of quieter people when it comes to the decision.

The Ways and Means articles listed under Step 8 (Let everybody know and ask them to be involved) are all relevant to creating interest in a review of school discipline. Creating and maintaining the interest and involvement of the school community is a process that needs to be continued throughout policy development and implementation.

Step 4: Decide whether or not to review your discipline policy

Now is the time to get the act together. All the discussion that has been going on in the various formal and informal groups has to be focused on answering the question: 'Should we review our present school discipline policy now?'

How you go about doing this depends on things like who started the ball rolling and how the school is organised.

Ideas:
- The principal may formally ask the staff, the parents, and the students to meet as a group and decide their recommendation.
- The school council may write to the principal, the staff and the students asking for their answers.
- A questionnaire may be sent out to all relevant people asking for their views.

In reaching the final decision, it is important to realise that:
- there must be a core of people who would be committed to carrying the idea through;
- if one important group is strongly opposed to the idea this may need to be discussed further before the final decision is made;
- the support of the principal is vital. The process of developing policy demands a lot of time, effort, resources like clerical help, and access to people and places. The principal, having the overview of the school's functioning, must be willing to support the idea.

If the decision is 'no' you should ask yourself 'why?' Perhaps
- existing policies and practices are working well;
- it is not the right time to go ahead;
- others do not see that discipline is an important issue to the school community;
- teachers are too busy with other duties to be bothered (although they may see the need);
- the existing climate of the school leads to a feeling of distrust and an unwillingness to work together.

If you still feel it is important to consider developing a policy, think about what can be done to have the idea accepted at a later date. (See the article 'Responding to resistance' in Ways and Means, Section 1.)

If you have made the decision to proceed with the process of developing a discipline policy, the next step is to plan carefully. Read on!

See Part Two: Ways and Means—

Section 1: Getting people working together
- Responding to resistance

Section 3: Surveys, observations and interviews
- Surveys

Section 4: Meetings and group discussions
- All articles

Guide to further reading

Should you wish to pursue some topics in more detail you may choose from an extensive list of books, films and videos, arranged under the following topic headings in Part Three of this book, References and Resources:
- Reports and general issues relating to discipline
- Behaviour management

Phase B
Plan

If you decide to go ahead with the review, planning is vital to ensure the best use of time, and the likely success of the project. Factors to be taken into account are:
- getting effective leadership;
- having clear decision-making procedures;
- involving the community.

People are more likely to implement a policy if they have had a say in it. It may seem that this involvement slows progress but effective consultation will have its pay-offs.

People develop valuable knowledge and skills and will quickly let you know if proposals are unacceptable.

Remember good ideas may come from previously untapped sources.

The following steps in the total process are seen as essential to this planning phase:

5. Determine who will organise the review.
6. Determine how decisions are to be reached in the review.
7. Plan how to proceed.
8. Let everybody know and ask them to be involved.

The outcome of going through these steps should be that a plan will have been made about:
- how the policy development will proceed;
- who will be involved and how;
- who will be responsible;
- a timeline.

Step 5: Determine who will organise the review

'None will improve your lot, if you yourself do not' — Bertolt Brecht

Somebody has to do the work. But who?

Since not even the principal can do it alone, a co-ordinating group (task force, project group, co-ordinating committee or mediation group) will need to be formed. Who should be in the co-ordinating group? Just any old group will not do.

Even an existing group may not be appropriate. A circumstance that may prevent effective planning in schools is that there are few traditional structures that actually help people work together to take responsibility for handling human problems.

Schools differ. Some are administered by a committee system, others have mini-schools, curriculum or subject streams. Some have a great deal of parent/community involvement and others have little. Some are in rural areas, and some are in the suburbs. Some serve localities where the people are very similar, others serve communities with ethnic or religious differences.

However, if you try to have a representative of every interest group in the school community in the co-ordinating group you will be sure to overlook and offend someone or have a group so large that you can never find a convenient time to have a meeting. Your task force therefore needs to be small enough to be workable, but comprised of individuals who can gain the co-operation and support of the various interest groups in your school.

Also, to be effective, the members must be credible people — active, intelligent, committed, and able to communicate effectively with one another and the local community. A good sense of humour is helpful.

A group of school staff may do the job, but experience has shown that a wider representation including, for example, parents and students provides a broader perspective for discussions, increases the likelihood that decisions will be accepted and helps with implementation.

Members can be appointed or elected, but to make sure that the 'right' people for your group are not 'left' out, semi-voluntary selection/election may be required, where people are gently pressured into the group because of past leadership performance or because they represent an important group within the school community (see Step 3).

See Part Two: Ways and Means—

Section 1: Getting people working together
- Mediation group model

Phase B

Step 6: Determine how decisions are to be reached in the review

In the development of a school discipline policy, three major areas need to be attended to:
- how decisions will be made;
- who is going to be involved in making them;
- gaining agreement that all members of the school community will abide by final decisions.

There are a number of ways of reaching decisions:
- by consensus
- by majority vote
- by averaging individual opinion
- by authority without group discussion
- by authority after group discussion
- by minority
- by the member with the most expertise
- by a delegate

Each of these methods may be appropriate on occasions. For example, staff may be quite happy if one person takes the initial responsibility for identifying resources for policy development.

But if no open decision is made about which method is going to be used at different stages in the policy development, then the risk is that some may consider proposals not binding on them because the decisions were not reached by 'fair' means or because they feel they were not asked.

Discussing important decisions widely ensures that people know what the issues are, provides individuals with an appreciation of the pros and cons, and generates a variety of alternative solutions. In general, it is wise to adopt the principle that if individuals or groups in the school community are going to be affected by the consequences of a decision they should, wherever possible, be given an opportunity to contribute to that decision.

Finally, an agreement must be reached that all members of the school community will abide by the final decisions about the discipline policy. (No white ants!) This is essential to ensure effective implementation.

It will be the responsibility of the co-ordinating group to ensure that these decisions are debated and taken.

See Part Two: Ways and Means—

Section 3: Surveys, observations and interviews
- Surveys
- Sample survey questions

Section 4: Meetings and group discussions
- All articles

Phase B

Step 7: Plan how to proceed

Planning does not always proceed in a neat, linear progression. Each group of planners and problem solvers develops its own pace and its own ways.

Write out the plan. Make it available. It acts as a blueprint for all to refer to so they can see where their tasks fit in with those of others.

The plan should set out what is to be done and how each step could be undertaken. State as clearly as you can the limits of what is required and give some suggestions about what methods could be used in going about tasks. However, the people who actually undertake the tasks should be encouraged to explore the various ways of doing things which they see as most appropriate for your particular school setting.

In effect, your plan is a summary of the process that will be undertaken to develop a policy statement. The stages and steps outlined in this book could be used as a framework for planning the process of development of a policy statement and a timeline could be attached.

Beware that the plan does not become the end in itself. A definite time limit should be placed on producing a plan.

A timeline is necessary since the scarcest resource in a school is time. Time for meetings in most instances must be found after school and/or at lunchtimes. Even with good agendas, careful preparation, outstanding chairing ability and good meeting skills, together with dedication by the staff, such meetings yield very few productive hours per year. The reality of a school operation is that many unanticipated events disrupt even the best-laid plans.

The plan and timeline then must be as brief and to the point as possible and flexible enough to respond positively to the unexpected. The need to cover the tasks effectively must be balanced against the need to ensure they are done quickly so that the process does not become bogged down or lapse.

A well-stated plan and timeline displayed publicly, perhaps on a noticeboard, with some means of marking off the tasks as they are completed, may breathe life into the process and stimulate and maintain interest in it.

See Part Two: Ways and Means—
Section 1: Getting people working together
- Team building

Step 8: Let everybody know and ask them to be involved

Two reasons for getting people involved are referred to in the John Cleese film *Decisions, Decisions* as 'reasons factual' and 'reasons psychological'.

Reasons factual:
- Valuable ideas and insights can be contributed by the collective wisdom of parents, students and others.
- If you overlook any group you risk developing a policy that is unworkable.

Reasons Psychological:
- People need to know about, accept and carry out a policy if it is to be of any use.
- They will know about a policy if they have had an invitation to contribute to its formation.
- They are more likely to accept it if they feel their viewpoint has been heard, even if some compromises are necessary in reaching the final decision.
- They are more likely to carry out a policy if they are committed to it. This commitment will come as people work through the process of development and get the feeling that the policy belongs to them.

An additional reason for involving people is that they will 'grow' with the policy. They will have a chance to reflect on attitudes to school discipline; they will be more fully aware of the reasons behind policy decisions; and they will gain knowledge needed to implement the policy.

How to go about it:

It may not be easy to get some people involved. You may have to overcome apathy or there may be people who are opposed to the idea of a review. Use a variety of formal methods to tell people about the review. You could, for example, distribute a circular, put articles in newsletters or the local newspaper, and talk to groups (school assemblies, classes, staff, school council, parent groups).

Some of the things people need to know are:

- How and why the school reached the decision to review its discipline policy. (You will need to sell the project by emphasising the benefits you expect, for instance, 'a happier school' or 'clear and sensible school rules'.)
- Why you want them to be involved. For example, 'We need to take into account the viewpoints of all staff, students and parents to develop the best policy for our school'.
- How you would like them to contribute. Outline your plans and the timeline and clarify the ways in which people will be asked to contribute.
- Who will co-ordinate the review.
- How decisions will be reached.
- Whom they can contact with any queries or suggestions. This may be the co-ordinators — or form teachers, parent representatives and others may agree to be nominated as contact persons.

Talk to people:
- Personal contact can be a powerful way of encouraging people to be involved. Informal conversations at lunchtimes and at social gatherings can be immensely valuable. You could either initiate a general conversation about discipline or discuss the review specifically. If you sense someone is opposed to the review, it may help to bring this opposition into

Phase B

the open by encouraging them to express their point of view.
- Telephone trees are a way of making personal contact with a large number of people. For example, parent representatives or teachers may each agree to phone a number of people to invite them to a meeting.

Use surveys, films or guest speakers:
- Surveys are discussed in the next chapter as a way of finding out about what is happening in the school. A survey can also help create interest and get people involved. They will need to think about discipline to answer the questions and they will probably be interested in hearing how other people answered the survey.
- Films or guest speakers are another way to raise interest in discipline. They need to be chosen carefully, as people can be put off if they think you are pushing a particular barrow. If people seem reluctant to turn up, you may need to link in with something else that you could expect to be well attended; hold a meeting when parents are collecting reports or when a new curriculum method or student options are being outlined.

See Part Two: Ways and Means—
Section 1: Getting people working together
- Outside consultants
- Circulars
- Making a video
- Discussion starters
- Responding to resistance
- Community meetings

Section 3: Surveys, observations and interviews
- All articles

Section 4: Meetings and group discussions
- All articles

Section 5: In-service education
- Guest speakers
- Films and videos

Guide to further reading
In addition to the references cited in the reading guide for Phase A, references relevant to the planning and organisation of a policy review can be found in Part Three: References and Resources, under the following topic headings:
- Leadership and the process of change in schools
- Evaluation
- Group participation in decision making (e.g. The John Cleese films *Decisions, Decisions* or *Meetings, Bloody Meetings* — practical advice from films that will also amuse you.)
- Parent and community participation
- Student involvement and responsibility in the school.

Phase C
Find out what actually happens in your school

Gather data. An accurate description of present discipline policy and practices is vital as a basis for deciding:
- what you value;
- what you want to keep;
- what you want to change.

A summary/report of this information is necessary:
- to provide a base for planning future action;
- to allow people who took part in the initial activities to see the results and know how they can contribute further;
- to allow all members of the school community to get the picture and think about their ideas in relation to others;
- to maintain interest and let people know that their views have been recognised.

The work that has gone into the review so far must not be allowed to go down the drain!

Phase C comprises the next five steps of the total process. These steps are:

9. Gather any policy statements that have a bearing on discipline.
10. Identify discipline practices used within your school.
11. Get reaction of parents, teachers, students to present practices and policies.
12. Find out people's expectations of school discipline.
13. Produce and distribute a progress report.

The outcome of going through these steps should be:
- Information will have been gathered about existing policies, practices and attitudes towards discipline in your school. A summary/report of this will have been produced.

Phase C

Step 9: Gather any policy statements that have a bearing on school discipline

Start with something concrete. Delve into the nooks and crannies of administrators' offices where you will be sure to find some current policy statements to help as a basis for your work.

As discipline is related to all aspects of school life your search for policies will need to be a broad one. You may find it helpful:
- to gather government, state-wide, regional, school and union policies;
- to examine your school's aims and objectives and judge whether their contents really are useful as a basis for your discipline policy;
- to explore up-to-date curriculum guidelines;
- to find the school's rules. Most schools have them and no doubt yours will have a lengthy list. This list may serve you well in the future.

Get multiple copies for your working group.

By the end of this stage you should have at your fingertips all existing policy documentation related to the topic. You are now ready to find out if the practice really reflects the policy.

18 Positive School Discipline: A practical guide to developing policy

Step 10: Identify discipline practices used within your school

It's all very well knowing what the discipline practices should be in your school, but do you know what in fact they are? Are people doing what they say they are doing?

You now need information about actual practices. This can be an exciting venture. It is often the first time that a school community talks about this issue.

Schools have found that using a variety of methods for gathering information has helped them to get a clear picture. Some of the techniques you could try include:

- observation;
- audio-taped or video-taped interviews with students;
- story writing or sentence completion by students;
- questionnaires.

Experience suggests that there is no such thing as a questionnaire to suit all purposes. While you may be able to borrow questionnaires, it is a worthwhile exercise for your working group to design its own. Remember you need to gather data from all sections of the school community. Everyone must have a chance to express their views.

Take care, however, not to gather more information than you need or can analyse.

Beware the temptation to evaluate the responses at this stage. That comes later. What you must do now is collate the information so that you can let people know as soon as possible what the main findings are.

See Part Two: Ways and Means—
Section 1: Getting people working together
- Discussion starters
- Making a video

Section 3: Surveys, observations and interviews
- Surveys
- Sample survey questions
  School and classroom discipline
  Analysis of school climate and organisation
- Observations
- Observation forms
- Interviews
- Gathering information from students
  (See also the articles cited in Step 11 and 12 which describe a variety of ways of conducting group discussions.)

Phase C

Step 11: Get reaction of parents, teachers and students to present practices and policies

If your school is like most others, your collated information shows some fascinating results. So now you need to report your finding back to the important groups (perhaps by mail, at a meeting or in a class discussion).

You will probably want to ask a range of questions about areas highlighted in your survey findings about, for example:
- teaching methods used;
- different discipline styles;
- what is taught and why and how this relates to discipline rules.

Useful questions are:
- 'What do these results mean?' (when students have listed 126 rules);
- 'What do you think we should do about this?' (when some parents say the strap should be kept);
- 'Is this policy out of date?'

You may also, during this process, decide to gather information on expectations about discipline (see Step 12).

On the other hand, you may find at this stage that members of the school community are, by and large, satisfied with the discipline policy and practices in existence. The steering group may then decide:
- to say there is no further need for action and to disband;
- to focus on any areas that need attention;
- to let the community know that there are alternatives worth their consideration.

See Part Two: Ways and Means—

Section 1: Getting people working together
- Community meetings

Section 2: Values clarification
- Describing school behaviour

- Voting with your feet

Section 4: Meetings and group discussions
- All articles

Phase C

Step 12: Find out people's expectations of school discipline

Ideas about how children should behave have changed dramatically over the last thirty years. The notion of 'children's rights' has emerged, elders are expected to earn, not command, respect, and young people are allowed to be more questioning. These factors can create tension in the school environment. The students' expectations about how they should behave may be based on peer-group and media views. Teachers' and parents' expectations may be based on what school was like when they were students. And the school will have its expectations about discipline at home.

Ideas about behavioural expectations must be gathered from all groups; you may use, for example, the 'Describing school behaviour' sheets, the 'Modified community conference technique' asking students to list and discuss behavioural expectations of teachers and compare these with their own ideas, or the 'Voting with your feet' exercise.

See Part Two: Ways and Means—

Section 3: Surveys, observations and interviews
- Sample survey questions
  See also the articles listed in Step 11.

An understanding of each group's expectations about behaviour is an essential basis of a discipline policy. The range of such expectations must be clarified before agreement can be reached on the aims of the policy.

Positive School Discipline: A practical guide to developing policy

Phase C

Step 13: Produce and distribute a progress report

Everyone will now need to know what you have found out. It is frustrating if too much time elapses before you inform people.

Use your progress report to summarise your main findings about school discipline policies and practices and people's expectations of school discipline. Highlight the practices that are valued, the areas of agreement and any issues of concern. Try to make your report brief and readable, perhaps using catchy summary headings. When it is completed, distribute your report as widely as possible in the school community.

It helps to get people together at this stage so that discussion can take place. People can really enjoy this process. They often find they are not the only ones who thought an issue important, or that some practices in current use were outmoded. If your findings indicate significant areas of disagreement you may need to plan strategies for the meeting to resolve or diffuse polarised opinion. Ideas for the future will emerge as people reflect on the findings, and discussion can be structured to lead directly into considering the earlier steps of Phase D (Agreeing on a framework and aims for your new policy).

In addition, see Part Three, under the following topic headings:
- Group participation in decision making
- Curriculum and teaching methods ... discipline
- Reports and general issues ... discipline
- School climate and organisation

See Part Two: Ways and Means—

Section 1: Getting people working together
- Circulars
- Community meetings

Section 4: Meetings and group discussions
- All articles

Section 6: Working out differences through discussion
- All articles

Guide to further reading

The references listed in Phase B are also applicable to this phase.

Phase D
Prepare your discipline policy

A written policy is an important step towards translating intention into practice.

Conventional wisdom tells us that in this phase you will need to consider:
- a framework to help you evaluate your current policy and to provide a guide for looking at options;
- aims and objectives;
- alternative ways of achieving your aims;
- acceptable options.

The necessary steps in the total process are:
14. Agree on the framework for your new policy.
15. Decide on the aims of your policy.
16. Explore a variety of ways of achieving your aims.
17. Select acceptable options.
18. Produce a draft policy.
19. Distribute draft policy for approval.

The outcome of going through these steps should be:
- A draft policy stating aims and objectives and detailing how these are to be achieved will have been written and distributed for approval.

Phase D

Step 14: Agree on the framework for your new policy

What will your discipline policy look like when it is finished? What areas will it cover? There are good reasons for asking these questions now. The answers will:
- provide direction for the activities that follow;
- give you a sense of where the task begins and ends;
- ensure that you are not suddenly confronted with major gaps in policy when the policy is implemented.

To develop a framework for the final policy the co-ordinating group should list the areas which it believes should be included.

If you already have a discipline policy and have been evaluating it as suggested you will know what areas are useful and what areas have been neglected in the past.

If you are starting from scratch the co-ordinating group could use the brainstorming process (see Part Two: Ways and Means) to get a list of areas. The next step is to put them in a logical order. Luckily, you don't have to re-invent the wheel completely. The following areas have been suggested by schools that have developed discipline policies:
- the school's aims and objectives;
- the school's definition of discipline;
- the goals of the discipline policy;
- positive programmes the school will adopt to achieve those goals;
- the responsibilities of teachers, parents and students in working towards those goals;
- procedures the school will adopt to resolve problems;
- specific roles of staff, parents and students in resolving problems;
- criteria by which the success of the policy will be evaluated;
- Departmental Regulations.

If your final policy says something about each of these areas it is likely to make a real contribution to making the school a better place for all.

See Part Two: Ways and Means—
Section 8: Aspects of positive discipline policies and practices
- All articles

See also Step 16 for ideas regarding the content of your policy, and the articles listed under Step 13 for strategies that may be useful in reaching agreement on a framework for your policy.

Step 15: Decide on the aims of your policy

In Step 11 you will have gained some understanding of what members of your school community believe about discipline and behaviour. You will have found differences and points of agreement. Now is the time to focus on the points of agreement. This will not be impossible because there is usually agreement that one of the ultimate goals of disciplinary approaches is to have students achieve control over their own behaviour. There will be other values on which most people agree (for example, respect for others, tolerance, cooperation, and trust) and these values can become the basis of your aims. They will be the rock on which your discipline policy stands or crumbles. For some assistance on the process of values clarification see Ways and Means, Section 2.

In developing aims, think of broad statements about the purpose of your discipline policy. Here are some examples of aims developed by other schools:

- 'We aim to establish acceptable patterns of behaviour and encourage in students the development of conscience, a sense of responsibility.'
- 'We aim to develop within students a strong feeling of self-worth.'

If your aims are clearly stated you will have a base from which you can develop specific practices and from which you can evaluate the success of your policy when it has been implemented.

See Part Two: Ways and Means—

All articles listed for Steps 13 and 14.

Luckily, you don't have to reinvent the wheel

Phase D

Step 16: Explore a variety of ways of achieving your aims

The time has come to find out what ideas are available on discipline and behaviour. You will be looking for models of behaviour and discipline systems that may answer the needs of your school. You will want to gather enough information to feel that your school is *au fait* with current thinking on the subject. This search will take time; time to find the information, time to distribute it and time to make sense of it. Where do you start? The following three questions may help you to focus your thoughts as you search for information and strategies.

1. How can we develop responsibility and self-discipline? This question implies long-term forward thinking about the behaviour the school wishes to promote in students. It recognises that schools can design carefully graded experiences to develop qualities such as self-confidence, self-discipline, respect for others and co-operation in students. It assumes that the development of positive personal and social behaviours should not be left to chance. In the jargon it represents a 'proactive' rather than a 'reactive' approach to discipline.

2. What changes can we make in curriculum, school organisation and environment to reduce the likelihood of behaviour problems? The curriculum we offer and the way we organise our school can sometimes have a negative impact on student behaviour. By making constructive changes to these areas we may be able to eliminate some problems at their source. Consider the impact of the following on student behaviour:

- What is taught
- How it is taught
- How students are assessed
- Timetabling and grouping
- Interpersonal relationships
- Welfare provisions
- Student involvement and responsibility
- The physical environment
- Relationships between school and home

3. What strategies can we use when problems do occur? Even in the best organised schools problems will occur. You will need to find a range of constructive ways of responding to disruption and conflict quickly and effectively.

Where can you find information and ideas on these three questions?

- Visit other schools and see how they have tackled the discipline issue. Ask what works and what does not.
- Read books that will give you an overview of theories of behaviour.
- Consult experts on behaviour management.
- Send selected staff to relevant in-service activities and make sure they report back.

There is so much information available. Remember you are looking for practices that fit your school and are based on principles your school community can accept. Don't forget you may find some of the answers right on your own doorstep. You may have effective practices which should be maintained. It is more economical to build on existing strengths than to start from scratch. It is also important for morale that you give recognition to things that are working well in the school and don't get too bogged down with problems. Look at your current policy in the light of the framework you have chosen for your new policy and decide what you are happy to keep.

· This step can also involve heated debate about the value of theories of behaviour. You may find someone saying, 'What's all this psychology nonsense? We need something practical'. Have your answer ready. If you're stuck, try this one:

Phase D

- 'Psychological theories describe common patterns of behaviour. They can help us to understand how people tick. If we know something about these patterns we are in a better position to bring about change in behaviour. Nothing is as practical as a good theory. We want to avoid relying on hunches and custom. We want to be systematic and effective.'

What theories of behaviour should you study? Wolfgang and Glickman (1980) and Charles (1981) give useful summaries of the main theories that will interest schools. They argue (and we agree) that teachers cannot afford to restrict themselves to one approach to behaviour. The same strategies may not be appropriate with all students at all times. Teachers are in a better position if they have a variety of strategies in their repertoire. Your school discipline policy may also draw the best ideas from a range of theories and systems.

During this stage you may want to run an in-service to keep everyone in touch with the information being gathered. In-service activities can have three possible outcomes. They can kill all interest in the subject, be fun but forgotten, or they can lead to a greater awareness and commitment to the task.

Don't forget to invite parents to the in-service. Arrange babysitting and interpreters if necessary or send a jargon-free summary home. Consider the ideas on running in-service programmes in Ways and Means.

See Part Two: Ways and Means—

Section 1: Getting people working together
- Outside consultants

Section 5: In-service education
- All articles

Section 6: Working out differences through discussion
- All articles

Section 7: Planning an approach to confrontations
- All articles

Section 8: Aspects of positive policies and practices
- All articles

Section 9: Rules and consequences
- All articles

Section 10: Discussion papers
- Is discipline a curriculum issue?

Phase D

Step 17: Select acceptable options

'**A**cceptable' means that your school community believes that the options chosen are valid, and are supported by a majority of people. In other words, they would support the use of these options in the school.

How can you select acceptable options? To start with, your planning group could get together with the list of options from Step 16 and look at each option in turn (for example, Glasser's approach to creating rules or Gordon's ideas on conflict resolution) considering:
- Is it a realistic option for your school?
- Will your staff be both willing and able to carry it out?
- What skills and resources will staff need?
- What advantages will this option bring?
- What problems or disadvantages will this option have?
- Would this option be consistent with the school's philosophy, aims and objectives, and with the aims for your discipline policy agreed upon in Step 15?

The planning group will then need to decide whether they are in a position to draft a policy statement or whether they need further consultation with the community (or groups within it) in order to select options that are likely to be supported by the majority of people. Commitments made in Step 6 about the way in which policy decisions are to be reached need to be considered at this stage.

Four further points:
- You should agree on what constitutes an acceptable majority.
- Common sense is always a good guide when looking for an option that will work.
- Beware the urgings of those who stand to benefit from one particular pet theory.
- Try to anticipate problems which may arise with the options you have chosen.

Plan ahead to minimise any areas of weakness.

See Part Two: Ways and Means—

Section 4: Meetings and group discussions
- All articles

Step 18: Produce a draft policy

Someone has to write the first draft. The task should be delegated to one or two people who have been involved in all stages of the data gathering process and have a clear understanding of the decisions that have been made to date, especially:
- the framework of the policy decided in Step 14;
- the objectives of the policy decided in Step 15;
- the options available to achieve the objectives that the school community will support.

The document will be most effective if expressed in clear, unambiguous language that faithfully represents what has been decided and if:
- responsibilities are specified clearly;
- tasks are outlined concretely so that people can be clear about what they are expected to do; and,
- evaluation procedures are included (see Step 20).

Step 19: Distribute draft policy for approval

Ideally, all the people who have contributed to the process to date should have the opportunity to read the draft and react to it. There are a number of ways of distributing the document:
- through the regular newsletters to the school community;
- via a special mailing;
- at a meeting convened for the purpose.

The school may need to arrange for translations of the draft for some members of the school community. It is important that student opinion is not overlooked during this reading and reacting phase.

Two crucial factors that should be allowed for are:
1. Time for all interested people to read and digest the draft statement.
2. Opportunity for all interested people to react to the draft statement.

Of these two, the second requires more thought:
- How will the reactions of each group be sought?
- Will students have class time for this?
- Will verbal or written comments be called for?

From the reactions, some fine-tuning of procedures or content may be necessary before you gain approval to test the policy on a trial basis.

See Part Two: Ways and Means—
Section 1: Getting people working together
- All articles

Section 3: Surveys, observations and interviews
- All articles

Section 4: Meetings and group discussions
- All articles

Guide to further reading

There is a vast amount of literature that could be relevant to your discipline policy. In addition to the references cited in Phase A, you may wish to select further reading from those listed under the topic headings below. We suggest you use consultants to guide your selection and to contribute to professional development sessions. See Part Three: References and Resources, under the following topic headings:
- Evaluation
- Curriculum and teaching methods as preventive approaches to discipline
- School climate and organisation
- Student welfare
- Interpersonal skills (for teachers)
- Assertion training (for teachers)
- Self-esteem, social skills and values clarification (for students)
- School rules
- Behaviour management

Phase E
Put the policy into practice

The preceding phases bring your school to the point of having a formal written discipline policy that has the agreement of the school community. However, this does not automatically guarantee that your policy will be translated into practice. In Phase E you will need to develop an implementation plan that bridges the gap between written procedures and action. An effective implementation plan will have such essential ingredients as an official implementation group, creative promotional strategies, skill development programs, and ongoing monitoring procedures.

The key steps of this crucial phase are:
20. Establish an implementation group.
21. Identify and provide skill development for all groups.
22. Launch and promote the policy.
23. Monitor practice.

The benefit of following these steps will be:
- Members of the school community will understand and use the policy. It will become part of the ongoing life of the school and it will be regularly reviewed.

Step 20: Establish an implementation group

Experience has shown that for a policy to be put into practice you need someone to take responsibility for making sure this happens. Ideally an implementation group will be formed to co-ordinate the introduction, maintenance, and monitoring of the policy. This group does not necessarily have to have the same membership as your original co-ordinating group. However, the same principles should be followed in determining appropriate membership (see step 5). Above all your group should have the authority, energy and support to allow it to do the job effectively. It certainly needs representation from the administration and should be firmly embedded in the existing organisational network of the school. The implementation group must be accountable to the school community. You should not be tempted to fob the job off to an existing committee that may be overloaded already.

Step 21: Identify and provide skill development for all groups

New policies often require members of the school community to review long held attitudes and ways of operating. Your discipline policy may advocate new approaches to communication, problem-solving, or conflict management. One of your implementation group's first tasks will be to identify any additional skills which community members will need to carry out the policy. Here we are talking about the skills needed by all groups affected by the policy — teachers, parents and students. Thus groups who have participated in the development of the policy then participate in programs to develop skills that will make the policy work.

At this point your implementation group may need to work within any guidelines the school has for the professional development of its members. Matching needs and programs will be an important step. There are many excellent programs available to assist your implementation group in its task.

Phase E

Step 22: Launch and promote the policy

It is essential that all groups within your school community fully understand the new policy and are aware of any implications for themselves. This awareness is only achieved by a careful process of communication that reaches all members of the school community.

There are many creative ways to publicise the policy. We suggest an actual launch — D-Day perhaps! You may devise signs, special lessons, and discussions, to affirm the importance of your policy. Some attention should be given to publicising the policy beyond the school in local papers or other media. These strategies can be used to give everybody credit for their participation in developing a policy that will make life in the school better for all as well as reinforcing the actual contents of the policy.

As part of a publicity campaign you should pay particular attention to the format of written documents. What documents will be needed for what purposes? There's no point in having a long-winded forbidding document that no-one will read. Summaries containing the main points of the policy are probably most useful. It is essential to have attractively presented documents prepared for students, teachers and parents, in language that they can understand.

To keep the policy in the forefront of people's minds after the initial launch you should plan opportunities for regular discussion. This may take the form of inviting comments at parent or staff meetings or from students in class meetings. These discussions can be built into the ongoing monitoring procedures and may alert you to the need for modifications or refinements.

Special attention will need to be given to providing induction programs for incoming groups of students, teachers and parents. They will need time to become familiar with the rationale and operation of the policy before they can also make a commitment to it.

Step 23: Monitor practice

The implementation group should plan for the monitoring and evaluation of the policy. There may be a need for a major review every few years however such large-scale reviews are time and energy consuming. We recommend smaller more frequent checks of different parts of the policy. Such ongoing monitoring allows a prompt response to any need for modification.

Criteria for evaluating the success of the policy will need to be established. Some of these criteria will be indicated by the original aims of your policy but other criteria will emerge. You may find unanticipated outcomes that are worth attention.

Some schools choose to develop a checklist of observations that could indicate the kind of changes you would expect if the policy were being followed. For example:
- students can identify the school rules
- teachers follow the procedures laid out in the policy
- teachers initiate problem-solving discussions with students when problems arise
- parents are involved in problem-solving conferences.

Asking people for opinions is another way of finding out whether or not the policy is working. Useful questions could be: "Are students working more happily in class?", "Do you think there is more agreement now between teachers, parents and students about suitable behaviour in school than there was before?"

During the monitoring process you should delegate specific tasks to particular individuals to carry out. A list of these tasks with a request for help could be circulated or put on a noticeboard.

The whole policy should not be discarded if shortcomings are identified; apply problem-solving processes to these shortcomings and develop modifications.

The time may come when a full-scale evaluation seems warranted. It is inevitable that as membership of a school community changes policies thought out and implemented by a different group of people become 'watered down' in practice, sometimes to the extent that they bear little resemblance to the original. This process of evaluation shares many of the attributes of policy creation. Again, it is important that all those affected by the policy are involved, and that the processes of creating interest, planning and information-gathering are gone through (see steps 1-13). Part Two of this book, *Ways and Means*, could be consulted for strategies to use at each step. Properly done, the process of evaluation can have all the benefits for a school that the initial policy writing did. It can rekindle enthusiasm and provide a renewed commitment to creating a positive learning environment.

See Part Two: Ways and Means

Section 3: Surveys, observations and interviews.
- All articles.

Guide to further reading

The hard work will be behind you at this stage and you may find it's time to devote your attention to issues other than discipline!

On the other hand this will be the time for some schools to further develop their policy. (Note that it can be practical to develop and implement different components of a policy sequentially). See Phase D reading guide.

Part Two:

Ways and Means

Section 1:
Getting people working together

The whole spirit of this book implies people working together for the common good. Perhaps this is easier said than done. This section in particular describes ways in which school communities can recognise individual opinions and encourage co-operation rather than conflict.

Lists of useful books, articles and some relevant films and videos to help mobilise the school community to work together on a policy development project can be found in Part Three of this book, References and Resources, under the following topic headings:
- Leadership and the process of change in schools
- Group participation in decision making
- Parent and community participation
- Student involvement and responsibility in the school
- School climate and organisation.

Section One

Team Building

Achievement of group goals is more likely if members of the group work as a team. A team may be two people (team teachers with one class), a group (the school council, a subject department), or a whole staff. However, a group of individuals rarely becomes a team without putting some conscious effort into the process. This does not have to take a great deal of time but, however long it takes, it will be time well spent.

When group members understand goals, are committed to them and 'own' them (that is, they see themselves as sharing and being responsible for them), they are likely to operate more effectively, experience greater personal and professional satisfaction and eliminate problems before they occur.

How do you develop a more effective team? Someone needs to chair the negotiations and facilitate the discussion. This role is not easy, although it sometimes appears easy, and may be most effectively taken by a person who is not part of the team. *(See 'Group discussions', in Section 4.)* It is this person's responsibility to assist the team to work through the following process:

Identify the team's goals
- Is there agreement within the team about the goals?
- Are all team members committed to the goals?
- Are the goals broken down into sub-goals?
- How will the team members know whether the goals have been achieved?
- Are the goals measurable?

Decide on programmes to achieve the goals
- Are these programmes clearly stated?
- Do team members understand their responsibilities in the programme?
- Is there consensus in the team about the programmes and team members' responsibilities?
- How will conflict be handled?

Identify skills of team members
- What skills, knowledge and resources are needed by team members to carry out the programmes?
- Is there a need for action, such as a training programme, to equip team members adequately?

Plan evaluation
- What evaluation procedures will be used?
- What data needs to be collected?
- What are the responsibilities of each team member in terms of evaluating the programmes?

Working through this process makes it easier for team members to monitor the progress of the team. This leads to more effective goal achievement, and enhances team members' feelings of involvement and satisfaction.

Mediation group model

It is neither desirable nor possible for one person to plan, develop and implement a school discipline policy. But to ensure that the job is done, it is essential that a group of people be identified clearly and given the responsibility. Without such a group, the discipline policy is likely to remain incomplete, not be implemented or prove ineffective. Naming this group a mediation group emphasises one of its central functions.

Among the most difficult elements in a process so long and complex are the many negotiations which must be made between people. It is usual for members of the school community to hold conflicting and, at times, apparently irreconcilable views, beliefs and values. However, for the school community to consider that they 'own' the policy in such a way that they will be prepared and able to implement it, they need to act together. Therefore, one of the most important and skilled tasks in the process will be that of negotiating and mediating between conflicting groups and individuals.

A mediation group, to be effective, must consist of active, credible, intelligent, committed people who can communicate effectively with one another and with the school community. Selection is essential. When we require special skills such as dentistry or mathematics teaching, we select for the special skills. We do not hold an election which is open to all interested parties. 'Guided democracy' may be necessary; suitably skilled members may need to be gently pressured to 'volunteer'.

Nevertheless, within those constraints, the members of the mediation group must in general be acceptable to the school community and mutually compatible.

Existing models and structures

Most schools use formal committees, or sub-committees, of administration, union or school council. However, a mediation or school community group that needs to work on more informal and personal lines is not a common structure; pioneering may be necessary in some schools. Formal committee meetings are no place for most of the negotiations and mediation that will need to be conducted by members of the mediation group in face-to-face communications — in the staffroom, classroom, playground, home or pub. Meetings in committee style should be reserved for in-service education, or presentation and discussion of material. Even then, personal contact and follow-up are essential.

Moving a school community from the beginning to the end of the process requires steady leadership as well as a good crew. Such a long, complex task is not for those with a casual interest. It requires a dedicated, self-generating commitment on the part of the people involved, since the actual undertaking of the process is not specified in the role descriptions of any one person — teacher, parent or principal. Their efforts must be carefully nurtured and supported by other members of the school community, including the principal.

Outside consultants

A school community can get positive assistance by inviting people from outside to contribute to their policy development process.

The outside consultant may:
- bring in new ideas gleaned from wide reading or working in schools;
- offer various alternative strategies for problem solving;
- help the school community clarify their ideas about what should be done;
- be able to put the school in touch with other resources;

- if well-known, attract interest from those previously uninvolved;
- by not being part of the regular school community, be able to run discussion groups, or write discussion material, without running the risk of the charge of self-interest to which a teacher or parent could be open; and
- act as a catalyst by being able to identify the concerns of different groups in the school; such a person could unite them in working towards solutions.

- school teaching staff
- school ancillary staff
- school council
- school parent clubs
- local council
- school support services
- regional office

Consider displaying some circulars in local shops so that interested others, perhaps parents of potential students, could offer a contribution. Think creatively about your community; could the senior citizens be involved?

Circulars

Circulars are a cheap and relatively easy way of contacting people as a start to getting them working together. The impact of circulars can be enhanced:
- if the message is clearly worded; readers need to know exactly what the request is;
- if recipients have sufficient information to be able to decide whether or not to participate; for example, if membership of a committee is required the number and times of meetings envisaged should be specified; people should be able to say 'no' gracefully;
- if a limited amount of material is set out on a page;
- if coloured paper is used;
- if translations, as appropriate, are provided;
- if it is clear how they are going to be sent out, and by whom; and
- if a regular day of the week is 'circular day'.

If each child is to be given a circular ensure that the teacher labels those for absent students and gives them out later. Important circulars could have a return slip to be signed by the parents to make sure that students deliver them.

The school could also draw up a circulation list; for example:

Making a video

Another way of getting people interested in policy development is through making a video. Parents and students alike enjoy seeing people they know on video.

Topics for such video discussion could include:
- ways to encourage students to work in class;
- appropriate clothes for school wear.

Rules for participants in the video must be clear beforehand:
- No names of people are to be used.
- No 'put downs' of persons present or absent will be allowed.

Make sure that both boys and girls participate in the discussion, and consider taping segments showing students from different year levels. Participants should have the opportunity to view the video before it is screened to others and request the removal of any parts to which they object.

By the way, good videos look simple but hide a host of difficulties. If you want to make one for public showing, have a practice run or two; you'll probably want to reduce the number in the group, the extraneous noise, and so on and so on . . .

Discussion starters

These questions were devised for discussion by small groups at a parent meeting; similar questions could be used in staff or classroom meetings or in informal interviews.

> In your small group please share your views on the following questions. There are no right or wrong answers. It is an opportunity for you to express your opinions on school discipline. Please ask someone in the group to take notes.
> 1. What behaviours do you believe the school should expect from students?
> 2. What behaviours do you believe are unacceptable at school?
> 3. What disciplinary procedures do you think have the most chance of success?
> 4. Do you think there are any ways this school could improve its approach to discipline?
> 5. If your child were experiencing discipline problems at school how would you like to be involved?
> 6. Do you think it important that school and home discipline should be similar?

Responding to resistance

When you are committed to seeing a positive discipline policy developed in your school, it can be discouraging to find that some other people are not so enthusiastic. Some groups or individuals may be hostile or openly cynical about your efforts, others may be apathetic or uninterested and some may promise support then not follow through. The question often asked by people leading or initiating a new project is, 'How do we cope with resistance?'

We can, in fact, be overzealous in interpreting all resistance as negative. If we recognise the positive side of resistance we can often respond to it more constructively. Active resistance can be a sign of energy to be harnessed. Defenders of the status quo may be able to help us avoid disaster by anticipating problems before they happen. Resistance also keeps us from the trap of accepting every new idea that comes along, of change for change's sake.

Section One

'We've tried it before; it won't work'

If your project is facing a cool reception, it's worth making time to take stock. Focus on trying to understand the dynamics of resistance with a view to reducing it, rather than opposing it. In most situations meeting resistance with opposition will increase it. Before working on solutions, think carefully about your own approach.

You could consider these questions:
- Can the people we want to get involved see a pay-off for putting time and energy into this project?
- Have we made the task seem too great, too overwhelming?
- Are we moving too fast for others to keep in touch?
- Are we 'coming on too strong'?
- Are we focusing on issues which reflect the real concerns of our school community?

The answers may lead you directly to possible ways of responding to resistance. The strategies below are only a few of the range of creative solutions you could generate:

- Invite participation of people affected by the project, through bulletins or word-of-mouth, to brief well-run meetings and discussion sessions.
- Use structured group processes to make your meetings productive (for example, 'Nominal group technique', see Section 4).
- Use social gatherings to get people involved in informal discussions concerning the project.
- Allow sufficient time for people to air their concerns during the process of developing a policy.
- Use as many media as possible to disseminate information about the project. Don't rely on one explanation.
- Publicise the benefits of the project for those affected.
- Use opinion leaders in the school community to 'spread the word'.
- Ask other people besides your co-ordinating committee to take an active role in the process — to visit another school and report back, or to read and summarise a relevant article for other staff.
- Trial small changes in classrooms of willing teachers and let the results speak for themselves (for example, classroom meetings).
- Provide appropriate training in new skills if these are required for teachers to successfully adopt new roles (for example, conflict management skills).
- Develop ongoing support for teachers trying new approaches (for example, through review meetings, reports, 'refresher' sessions, team teaching).

To sharpen your understanding of the

possible range of reactions to an innovation you may like to read about the 'Concerns-Based Adoption Model' (CBAM) developed by Hall, Wallace, Dossett (1973) at the Texas Research and Development Centre for Teacher Education *(see part Three: References and Resources)*.

This model describes the different feelings and attitudes individuals may hold towards an innovation. Research on the CBAM model has identified seven stages of concern:

0. I'm not interested. (Awareness)
1. What is involved? What's it about? (Information)
2. How will it affect me? (Personal)
3. How do I do it? (Management)
4. How will it affect the students — How can it work better? (Consequence)
5. How can we work together to make this more effective? (Collaboration)
6. Is there an even better way? (Refocusing)

Knowing where individuals or groups stand in relation to your project may help you to develop strategies that are more effective because they match the level of concern of the individual or group. Hall (1979) suggests some strategies which may be appropriate to the seven levels of concern.

Experience in working towards change in school communities shows us that initiators of projects need to possess many qualities:
- an understanding of human nature;
- a belief that change is possible;
- an acceptance that real change (behavioural and attitudinal) occurs slowly and not always smoothly;
- an ability to set up effective channels of communication;
- creativity, to design ways of arousing interest without activating resistance;
- an ability to influence and get active support from key people;
- an ability and a willingness to work alongside others;
- a sense of humour.

As few of us are superhuman we usually need to work with a group of people who can share our enthusiasm, help us overcome the difficulties and, we hope, enjoy the results of getting a new and positive policy into operation.

Community meetings

You will be bound to need several community meetings in the course of developing your discipline policy. They can enable a large number of people to contribute to the policy and also help develop skills and knowledge that will be of value to implementation. Carefully planned and conducted meetings lead to more productive outcomes so time spent here is time well spent.

Planning

Decide on the purpose of the meeting
For example:
- To encourage community members to express and clarify their attitudes to school discipline.
- To enable the community to contribute to decision making regarding sections of the policy.
- To introduce a number of theories of behaviour management and to encourage discussion of these theories.

Decide whom to invite

Creative thinking is called for to entice tired parents out at night and, remember, parents will be more motivated to attend a meeting if they can see that the topic directly concerns their children. If you think a general invitation may not get a great response, consider other ways; for example, rather than aiming for all families to be represented, some schools pick a representative from each level.

Section One

Communication can go like this

principal
↓
class teacher
↓
class parent representative(s)
↓
who attend meeting and then contact
↓
all parents of class
↓
students

Another version is

organising group
↓
principal
↓
class teachers
↓
students
↓
parents

One school that decided to hold a discipline night got all the children to write an invitation (RSVP) to their parents. The weekly newsletter gave more information. The response was overwhelming. The format of the meeting was determined by the school council and the discipline committee. It was decided to have short talks from the principal, an external facilitator, some small- and whole-group discussion and a film. The multi-purpose room was overflowing and discussion was difficult to complete in the allocated time. The parents unanimously asked for more.

Decide on the format and agenda

The format may include:
- a warm-up activity
- small-group discussions/workshops
- large-group discussions
- films
- guest speakers
- a refreshment break

It will be important that as many people as possible have an opportunity to express their opinions. Small-group discussions are better suited to this purpose than large-group discussions.

Other articles in this or the following sections — on group discussions, choosing a guest speaker, making a film or video, for example — may assist you in choosing the best format *(see Section 4, in particular).*

Choose a time and venue

Choose a time and venue that suits your community. You may even need to hold two meetings. Of course, the venue needs to have space and equipment for the activities you plan. Preferably, it will be attractive and comfortable and have facilities for refreshments. Because the school environment can be inhibiting to some participants, some people think it is better to hold meetings elsewhere.

Before the meeting the organisers have several important tasks:

Advertise the meeting

Be clear about the purpose of the meeting, its agenda and what people will be expected to do. For example:

46 Positive School Discipline: A practical guide to developing policy

'We would like you to attend the meeting so that you can be involved in choosing the right discipline policy for our school. At the meeting you will be asked to form groups of six people and discuss these questions:
- What could be done to prevent discipline problems?
- What should be the goals of our discipline policy?

The ideas generated will be collated and will help us draft goals and general strategies for our discipline policy. We will send you a summary of discussion notes.'

Use more than one method
- A notice on a board is likely to be ineffective; a circular is better.
- Word-of-mouth through a child is very effective, and personal contact by the principal, a staff member or a parent representative will normally produce results.
- If necessary, send out your circular in different languages and arrange to have interpreters at the meeting.

Organise essential details
- Guest speakers need to be briefed.
- Furniture, equipment, materials and refreshments need to be organised.

Smooth conduct of one meeting can encourage participants to come again. When the meeting starts someone should welcome all participants, introduce the organisers and clarify the purpose and agenda of the meeting. Procedures followed during the meeting will depend upon the format you have chosen. At the end of the meeting the chairperson should thank participants and assure them that their contribution will make a difference. They should be promised a summary of any discussion of workshop notes and that they will be kept informed of progress in developing a discipline policy. Participants could also be invited to make further comments after the meeting; a drop-in time and/or a suggestion box could be organised.

Follow up of the meeting is essential to maintain the involvement and motivation of participants. Notes should be summarised and distributed as promised. This will let people see that their views have been noted and will help them reflect on the proceedings. The permanent record of the meeting will also be a useful reference at the time of drafting the policy and at subsequent reviews.

Notes should also be distributed to non-participants so that they can find out what happened and be encouraged to attend future meetings.

Making official documents matter

People cannot reasonably be expected to follow policy if they don't know what it is. Because there are rarely enough copies of official documents to go around, schools need to develop systems of information location. For example, it should be known that there will be a copy of each new document:
- with the principal
- in the staffroom
- in the library
- with the school council

Notice of each new document could be given at staff meetings or, better still, in writing. (Some schools have pigeon holes for staff and school council mail.) The responsibility for reading the document then rests with the individual person. Summaries of lengthy documents can alert people to the importance of documents and encourage them to read the whole thing.

At the beginning of the year, all staff could be given a list entitled 'Where to go when you want to know'. Such a list sets out, under headings, the location of important information; for example, Gazettes, Regulations, policy statements.

Section 2:
Values clarification

In any school community there is likely to be a range of views on discipline issues. Discussions about discipline in schools will inevitably tap people's beliefs about what behaviour is desirable and acceptable, what motivates human behaviour and how behaviour can be changed. Clearly, people do not always agree on how children should behave and how they should be managed.

To omit consideration of values and attitudes in developing a discipline policy is to invite problems and to reduce the probability that enough people will actually practise what the policy preaches. There are many stages in the discipline policy process where failure to acknowledge value issues can lay a minefield of subsequent problems.

A school community could fall into the trap of searching for disciplinary strategies without having worked out a definition of 'discipline' which includes statements and goals acceptable to members of that community.

It is likely, if time is allocated, consensus can be reached about the goals of a discipline policy. For example, most people will agree that the development of self-control in students is one goal worth supporting. However, it may be less easy to reach agreement about which strategies will help achieve such goals. An example of a controversial strategy is the use of negotiating and contracting with students to solve problems. Some people will argue that negotiation is a desirable and effective way to deal with problems, others will argue the opposite. A range of beliefs about the maturity of students, the role of a teacher and the value of negotiation might underlie these different positions.

Failure to actually use such discipline strategies as negotiation can often be traced to the reluctance of people to support a strategy which is in conflict with a strongly held value or belief, or a feeling that their own views have not had a fair hearing.

Raising value issues for discussion is therefore a very important part of the process of developing a discipline policy. Five activities that can be used for this purpose are included in the following pages. It is best to start in areas where there is likely to be some

Section Two

agreement. Asking questions like 'How do we want students/teachers/parents in our school community to behave?' can get discussion started in a constructive way.

With more controversial issues it is possible to develop a climate in which differing values can be expressed with tolerance and without rancour. Although it is always difficult to change people's values and attitudes it may be possible to find points of agreement once the issues are opened up for discussion. *(See 'Voting with your feet'.)* On some occasions it will be possible to identify creative solutions to disagreements using processes like 'brainstorming'.

In areas where no agreement can be reached, the school community will need to address the issue of how differing values and viewpoints can be accommodated and respected. You may find it helpful to use some of the discussion papers from Section 10.

What do we mean by 'discipline'?

There are a variety of possible interpretations of the word 'discipline'. These range from the idea of discipline as an educative process to equating discipline with punishment. If people in your school community don't have a shared understanding of what discipline means, confusion, conflict and resistance may result. You may find your efforts to develop policy disintegrate into emotional arguments about humanistic versus authoritarian approaches as people entrench themselves in their preferred camp. Therefore it is important to spend time coming to an agreement about what 'discipline' means to your school. The following definitions and descriptions of discipline may provide a useful starting point for your school community to develop its own definition.

Some schools as a result of such discussions have chosen to avoid the word 'discipline' and to title their policy a school or student welfare policy.

Definitions for discussion

- Instruction imparted to disciples or scholars; teaching; learning; education; schooling.
- Instruction having for its aim to form the pupil to proper conduct and action; the training of scholars or subordinates to proper and orderly action by instructing and exercising them in the same; mental and moral training.
- The order maintained and observed among pupils.
- A system or method for the maintenance of order, a system of rules for conduct.
- Correction; chastisement; punishment inflicted by way of correction and training.

— **The Oxford English Dictionary,** Clarendon Press, Oxford, 1933

- *Discipline involves two ideas: on one hand, control, and on the other, punishment. While the idea of discipline does not necessarily mean physical punishment, that is what it has come to mean for many people . . .*

— Jane and James Ritchie, **Spare the Rod,** George Allen and Unwin, Sydney, 1981

- *School discipline is the functioning of the school community through a system of relationships, rules, rewards and sanctions designed to develop progressively self-discipline within students.*

— **Self Discipline and Pastoral Care** (Thomas Report), Education Department of New South Wales, 1981

- *Discipline may be recognised as the process whereby student and staff relationships are structured to maximize the educational, social and emotional well-being and attainments of students, to attain the most effective and efficient use of human and material resources and to facilitate the maximum satisfaction of needs for all members of the school.*

— **Discipline in secondary schools in Western Australia,** (Dettman Report), Education Department of Western Australia, 1972

What is important to me?

The checklist below can be used with groups of teachers and/or parents as a values clarification activity.

1. Introduce values clarification as an important step in developing a discipline policy.
2. Provide all participants with a copy of the checklist.
3. Ask participants to individually rank the ten values they would most want their students/children to share (ranking 1-10). Ask them also to rank the ten values they believe are least important (rank 31-40).
4. Place participants in small groups with a discussion leader to discuss their choices. Stress that the aim is to share reasons for choices, not to change opinions.

Section Two

5. Following discussion, group leaders tally priority values for the group to get the top ten. Group tallies can then be completed to identify the ten most important values for the school community.
6. A valuable follow-up activity is to get small groups to consider how the school might actively promote its top ten values. Each small group could work on one or two values using the brainstorming process to generate ideas.

Values clarification — what is important to me?

Our values affect all of our behaviour. Think of your students/children growing up to be adults. What qualities do you want them to value, both now and in the future? Rank the ten that you consider to be most important (1-10) and the ten that you consider to be least important (31-40).

I want my students/children to value:

Happiness	Honesty	Humour
Freedom	Loyalty	Trust
Rules	Democracy	Thoughtfulness
Individual dignity and worth	Respect for authority	Dependence
	Competitiveness	Being liked
Efficiency	Tolerance	Self-reliance
Smoothing over trouble	Caring	Ambition
	Caution	Assertiveness
Difference	Openness	Confidence
Initiative	Self-awareness	Spontaneity
Tradition	Individuality	
Originality	Politeness	
Responsibility	Security	
Courage	Conformity	
Independence	Obedience	
Intelligence	Co-operation	

---

52 Positive School Discipline: A practical guide to developing policy

Describing school behaviour

It can be difficult to put into words what you value in children's behaviour. A three-step activity is suggested here. It can be used with individuals or with people working in small groups. In practice, you would need to type out the instructions onto three separate sheets and copy them for each person.

Step one

We all have ideas about how students should behave in school. However, when different members of the school community are working to develop a discipline policy they need to agree on what they see as desirable behaviour.

As a first step, it is useful to list actual observable behaviours. Here are some examples:
- Students stay quiet when teacher is talking.
- Students put up their hands when they want to ask a question.
- Students answer when spoken to.

Add your list below:

Section Two

Step two

If you put together all the suggested desirable behaviours, a very long list would result. Consequently, most people group the behaviours and come up with a summary statement like this:

Behaviours	Summary
1. Stays quiet when teacher is talking.	Keeps classroom rules
2. Puts up hand to ask a question.	
3. Answers when spoken to.	

Task:
Group the behaviours you listed on Sheet One so that you can make summary statements about them.

Step three

Although it is not too difficult to list the sorts of behaviours that we think students should demonstrate in school, it is not always so easy to understand why these are important to us. Sometimes behaviours are listed because they were the ones expected in our school days and we feel comfortable with them. Or behaviours are listed because of some strong belief such as 'children should be seen and not heard'. When it comes to members of a school community needing to agree on acceptable behaviours it helps if they each understand what others value when they put something on the list. To help clarify these beliefs, write down your summary statements and then ask 'Why is that important?' like this:

Summary	Why important
1. Keeps classroom rules	So that the teacher can get on with teaching.
	Because children should do as they are told.

54 Positive School Discipline: A practical guide to developing policy

Section Two

Voting with your feet

This activity helps clarify values and attitudes and provides an active way of initiating discussion about views on discipline.

> 1. Gather five or six statements on discipline that are likely to elicit differing opinions.
>
> For example:
> - If a student misbehaves he needs understanding rather than punishment.
> - Students should be given reasons for the restrictions put upon them.
> - Fear is a desirable method to use in controlling the behaviour of students.
> - Physical punishment is the only thing that some children understand when they disobey.
> - Matters of discipline should be decided by the teacher and student together.
> - Corporal punishment is a necessary discipline strategy in schools and should be reintroduced.
> - Students should be allowed to make their own decisions.
> 2. Set up the following five positions on a continuum around your meeting room — strongly agree, mildly agree, neutral, mildly disagree, strongly disagree.

Positive School Discipline: A practical guide to developing policy 55

Section Two

3. Introduce the activity as an opportunity for participants to share and discuss their views on discipline issues. Stress that it is expected that views will differ on some issues and that the aim of the activity is to open discussion, not to change points of view. Ask participants to select and move to their position in response to each statement without discussion. Encourage participants to make a choice and use the 'neutral' category sparingly.

4. Read the first statement to the group and allow time for participants to move to their selected position.

5. Allow time for participants to discuss the reasons for their choice with participants who have chosen the same group.

6. Record numbers of participants in each position on a chart.

7. Repeat steps 4-6 for each statement.

8. At the conclusion of this process you have two options:
   - Either conduct a discussion, in one large or several small groups, about the profile recorded on the chart, or
   - ask participants to take up their positions again on the statement on which the chart shows there was an equal division of opinion. Form two groups representing 'agree' and 'disagree', then develop pairs across these two categories. The pairs should then undertake the following exercise:

   (i) Label partners A and B.
   (ii) A states own position and why it is held.
   (iii) B summarises A's position, 'You believe that . . .'
   (iv) A corrects summary if necessary.
   (v) B states own position.
   (vi) A repeats process.
   (vii) Allow the exercise to continue for ten minutes so that both A and B feel they have expressed their views.

Memories of school

This activity is designed to allow school community members to reflect on their own school experiences as a basis for clarifying their values towards schooling and desirable student management practices. The activity is a good warm-up at the beginning of an in-service programme and can be used with large groups. If necessary, the school could seek the help of an experienced group facilitator or consultant to advise or conduct this activity and others in an in-service programme.

Strategy:
- Each person is asked to silently recall a positive and a negative experience at school.
- In groups of four, participants share experiences and find words or phrases to summarise their experience.
- In the whole group the leader writes up these words in two columns and leads a brief discussion on implications.
- Discussion starters:
1. Which were easier to recall — positive or negative experiences? Why?
2. What were the typical areas of experience remembered — for example, teacher-student relationships, teacher qualities, student-student relationships, achievements and failures?
3. What experiences do we want our students/children to repeat/avoid?

Section 3:
Surveys, observations and interviews

In each phase of developing a positive school discipline policy you will need to gather information, opinion and suggestions from the various sections of your school community.

The better the strategies you devise for doing this, the sounder the basis you will have for decisions about your new policy. No one method is recommended over the others; each has its advantages and limitations.

In this stage you need to be careful not to go overboard. Information gathering should not become an end in itself. It is a matter of finding the balance between alienating people by not asking their opinion or asking too much and ending up with a flood of unusable data. We've all been left frustrated and annoyed by spending time answering surveys and questionnaires never to hear the results. Therefore you should aim to keep your information-gathering strategies brief and to the point. You should always ask yourselves the critical questions:
- What information do we need in order to proceed?
- How do we plan to use this information?
- How will the data be analysed?
- What questions, therefore, will we ask?

Section 4 describes further data-gathering strategies, each involving some form of structured group discussion.

Section Three

Written surveys

Some of the advantages of written surveys are:
- They are a relatively quick way of exploring the opinions of a large number of people, in comparison, for example, with personal interviews.
- Some people may give an opinion in writing, but be reticent in public; for example, in class or staff meetings where a few people can dominate discussions.
- People can answer anonymously if they choose.
- If you work in a climate where sceptics may discount your results, it's safer to have a hard copy of people's answers than to make your own notes in interviews.

Some of the disadvantages of surveys are:
- Usually, less information can be obtained than in discussion, because it's not possible to ask people to clarify or elaborate on a response.
- Some people may be reluctant or unable to write down responses. It may be better, for instance, to interview young children, and to avoid mailed surveys generally because response rates to these are typically very poor.

Writing questions

Keep the questions clear and unambiguous.

Make the meaning of your question as clear as possible. You may be surprised how many different interpretations can be given to apparently simple questions. For example, possible answers to the question 'Where were you born?' are 'Australia', 'Mercy Hospital' or 'Berwick'. Clearly, the level of detail required needs to be specified in the question.

Avoid asking people to respond to more than one concept at a time.

For example, 'Do you agree with A and B?' A common double-barrelled question is, 'Would you like tea or coffee?' The answer, 'Yes please', doesn't tell the questioner what he wants to know.

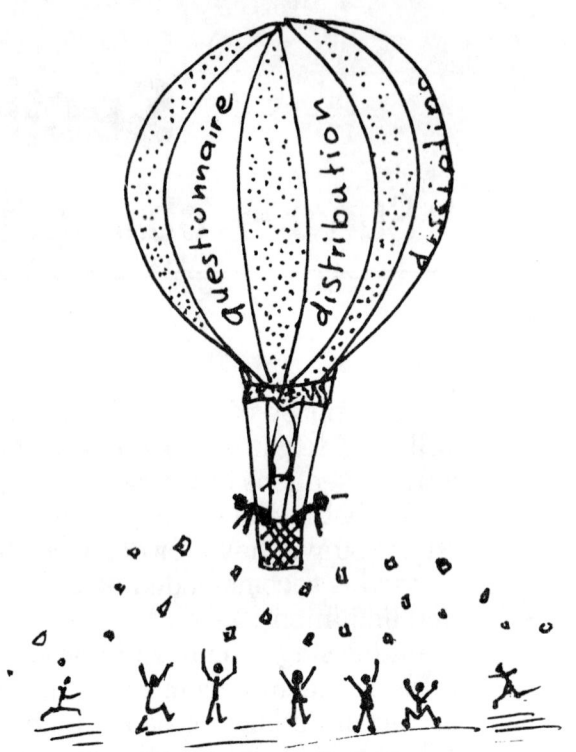

Consider a variety of forms of questions.

Open-choice questions allow people to compose their own reply. Forced-choice questions specify the possible alternative responses and ask people to mark the one that is best for them. A forced-choice question is easy to collate and generally makes it clear to everyone what information is required. If it is possible to specify the alternative answers to a question, it will be a more reliable means of finding out what you want to know.

On the other hand, forced-choice questions place a limit on the information you can gain and they can be irritating. Do try to avoid forcing people to choose between answers that do not truly reflect their beliefs or situation. Above all, make sure your survey has sufficient open-ended questions to allow people to make suggestions and to fully explain their point of view if they wish to.

Rating scales are a particular form of forced-choice question. For example:

Section Three

> 'To what extent do you agree with each of the following statements?'
>
> **Statement:**
> Students should be sent home if they fight.
>
> | Agree | Agree to some extent | Disagree to some extent | Disagree |
> |---|---|---|---|
> | | | | |

Notice that people were not given the option of 'sitting on the fence' in this example. If given the opportunity, many people will pick a neutral answer where in fact they do know which side of an issue they are more in agreement with. The advantage of removing the middle point needs to be balanced against the possibility of annoying the respondents.

Ask yourself: 'Is the survey free from bias?'

It is difficult to avoid bias in a survey. Here are two questions that may help you judge yours: 'Does it genuinely ask for opinions and suggestions or is it merely asking for support for an opinion you have already formed?' 'Does it allow people to identify positive features of the school as well as concerns?'

Don't make the survey too long.

Consider the time commitments and concentration span of your respondents. If a survey looks too long or too difficult, people won't reply.

Conducting the survey

Have a pilot run.

It is essential to trial a survey. Ask pilot subjects if they found any questions difficult to answer and if they would add or delete any questions.

Ensure a high return.

Try to get at least 80 per cent of your target group to complete the survey. One idea would be to hand it out at a meeting where all are present and have them return it to a box before leaving. It may be appropriate to give advance notice of questions.

If you can't use the above approach, then expect to put time and effort into encouraging people to return the survey. Experience suggests that two or three deadlines will be needed.

Ensure confidentiality.

Unless you really need people's names, let them answer anonymously. You may need a separate list to keep track of who has returned the survey.

Give feedback as soon as possible.

Try to give people a summary of results as quickly as possible after enough surveys have been returned.

Ways to use surveys

Survey teachers to find out:
- what discipline practices are used in the school;
- how effective teachers think those practices are;
- whether they have any suggestions or requests concerning school discipline;
- what they regard as significant discipline problems in the school;
- how they establish rules in the classroom;
- their attitudes to discipline (see Section 2: *Values clarification.*)

Survey students to find out:
- what they believe to be the school rules;
- how they rate different discipline strategies.

Some sample survey questions have been given in the following pages. Although these or similar questions have been used in other schools we recommend that you trial and modify them to best suit your own school.

Further examples of survey questions can be found in the works of Blachford (1984), Cohen and Harrison (undated), Fox et al (undated), Wayson et al (1982) and Williams and Batten (1983), all of which are listed in fuller detail in Part Three: References and Resources.

Section Three

Sample survey questions
School and classroom discipline

These questions have been written for teachers, but you could consider modifying them for pupils. In either case we suggest they are answered anonymously.

1. **How often do you use the following discipline strategies?**

	Very often	Frequently	Sometimes	Rarely

   - Withdraw a privilege (e.g. a special activity)
   - Ignore disruptive behaviour
   - Verbally reprimand student(s)
   - Teach or explain appropriate behaviour
   - Send student to principal
   - Send student to co-ordinator
   - Send student to corridor
   - Send student to a 'corner' or other separate part of the room
   - Reward appropriate behaviour
   - Reward disruptive students when they are good
   - Detain individual students
   - Detain whole class
   - Talk individually with child
   - Issue threats
   - Ensure that disruptive students are coping with their work
   - Notify parents
   - Discuss with parents
   - 'Hands on heads'
   - Plan interesting lessons
   - Negotiate teaching goals or methods
   - Make friends with difficult students
   - Discuss rules with class
   - Give lines
   - Negotiate an agreement that is acceptable to both teacher and pupil
   - Set unpopular tasks
   - Give extra responsibilities to difficult students
   - Plan plenty of activities to keep students busy
   - Use 'house points' or other token economy schemes
   - Other (please specify strategies that you use)

2. **How effective do you think these discipline strategies are?**

	Very effective	Moderately effective	Little or no effect	Counter-productive

   - Withdraw a special privilege (e.g. special activity)
   - Ignore disruptive behaviour etc. (Repeat of above list)

62 Positive School Discipline: A practical guide to developing policy

Section Three

3. Classroom rules

3.1 How are your classroom rules decided?
- The teacher decides. ☐
- Teacher decides after some discussion with students. ☐
- Teacher and students negotiate rules. ☐
- The students decide. ☐
- Other (please specify): ☐

3.2 Have the classroom rules been made explicit?
- Yes ☐
- No ☐

3.3 How is your class made aware of classroom rules? (Tick one or more boxes)
- Through 'general expectations' of teachers ☐
- Through discussion of rules with the students ☐
- Through the teacher telling the class ☐
- Rules are displayed on charts or in a rule book ☐
- Other (please specify): ☐

3.4 Are there specific consequences for breaking specific rules?
- Yes — for all rules ☐
- Yes — for some rules ☐
- No ☐

If yes, have these consequences been made explicit?
- Yes — for all rules ☐
- Yes — for some rules ☐
- No ☐

4. Student behaviour

4.1 Please describe any concerns you have regarding student behaviour in this school.

4.2 Please describe any positive features of our students' behaviour.

5. Discipline Strategies

5.1 Please describe any concerns you have regarding discipline practices in this school.

5.2 Please describe any discipline practices in this school that you are happy with.

6. Do you have any further comments or suggestions to make concerning school discipline?

Positive School Discipline: A practical guide to developing policy

Section Three

Analysis of school climate and organisation

Below is a list of factors that may either contribute to or help prevent school discipline problems. Please comment briefly on how you see these factors affecting discipline in our school. Indicate clearly which particular aspect of the school you are thinking of — for example, 'Playground: Not enough sheltered areas for outside play. Students fight for the better positions — are generally cranky on cold/wet days'.

Please try to think of both positive and negative aspects of our school. You may find you wish to identify both positive and negative aspects under the one heading.

1. Physical environment
- Playground environment

- Spatial arrangement of classrooms, meeting rooms, corridors, office, etc.

- Classrooms

- Overall appearance of school

- Other

2. School organisation
- Timetabling

- Grouping of students

- The way decisions are reached

- 'Welfare' provisions of the school
  (e.g. home-teachers, counselling)

- Other

3. Curriculum
- Curriculum goals

- Teaching methods

- Extra-curricular activities

- Assessment methods

4. Teacher attitudes and behaviour
- Teacher attitudes and behaviour towards students

Section Three

- Teacher attitudes and behaviour towards each other

- Teacher modelling of appropriate or inappropriate behaviour

5. School rules and discipline procedures
- School rules

- Discipline procedures

6. School-community relationship
- Parents' involvement in the school

- Other community members' involvement in the school

- School projects in the community

Clarifying roles and responsibilities

Asking parents and teachers to complete the statements below might be useful in clarifying the roles and responsibilities of various members of the school community in relation to discipline. Similar questions could be developed for the school administration, co-ordinators or students. These questions could be used in surveys, interviews or discussion groups.

Sample questions
For teachers
1. The responsibilities I take in relation to discipline are:
2. I think my colleagues expect me to take the following roles in relation to discipline:
3. The kinds of help I would like from —
    (i) colleagues
    (ii) administration
    (iii) parents
    (iv) consultants
    in relation to discipline are:
    (i)
    (ii)
    (iii)
    (iv)

For parents
1. As a parent I would like the school (teachers and administrators) to take the following responsibilities in relation to school discipline:

Section Three

2. I think I have the following responsibilities in relation to school discipline:

3. I think the school expects me to take the following responsibilities in relation to school discipline:

Observations

If Fleming discovered penicillin by noticing mould growing, just imagine what you might start by looking carefully as you work in a school. (If you follow up of course with some thoughtful self-questioning.)

For example: What games are students playing during break? What idle - mischievous things are they doing? Which students are involved?

What time of day do incidents happen? In which particular classes? Are some days always worse than others? Are some days better than others?

One or two observations made informally could be used as interest generators. For example: 'After Monday morning assemblies, when students learn how many house points they gained last week, we rarely have a student sent to the office during the rest of the day. Do other staff members also find Monday relatively trouble-free?'

Or an initial observation may be used to get others involved in gathering further information: 'I noticed Kerry missing from class on Friday afternoon. Were there any other students missing at the same time? What about previous Friday afternoons?'

Observations can also be made in more sophisticated ways, perhaps by using checklists or agreed-upon forms to fill in. Some may be concerned with gathering data about the way time is spent (for example, how much time elapses with students all working); or whether particular types of incidents occur more frequently at certain times of the day, and in specific locations around the school.

A word of warning about making observations: it is very easy to make inferences about what you see and hear. For example, two people observe the same incident and report it thus:

Person 1:
- Robin offended Lee.

Person 2:
- Robin said to Lee, 'You're a stupid idiot'.

Section Three

Sample observation forms

The following two observation sheets were prepared by teachers at an I.S.E. activity in the Shepparton area.

Instruction to teachers

Aims
- To gain a factual data base.
- To assist in finding the major discipline problem areas in the school and thereby . . .
- To assist in establishing a uniform discipline procedure in the school.

Further information:
- During a specific week of school, staff members will be asked to complete a personal copy of this survey sheet for each working day.
- Sheets will be stapled to absence slips each morning so that all form teachers will have their copies readily available.
- All other teachers will be issued with their sheets daily.
- Boxes will be supplied in the respective staffrooms for receipt of completed sheets at the end of each day of that week.

Specific week . . . . to be notified.

Although these observation lists focus on negative behaviour they are used to generate positive outcomes — to demonstrate a clear need for action to prevent specific behaviours, for example, or to urge consideration of ways in which teachers and students relate to each other. Their use in practice can also demonstrate that the discipline problems in the school are actually far fewer than has been the general impression.

Another approach to observation was taken by Chelsea Heights Primary School. As part of the process of evaluating their school discipline policy they decided that each teacher would record observations of both positive and negative happenings in the school during one particular week.

Instructions to the teachers and the two forms they used to record their observations are reproduced on page 72.

Note that they recognise that the causes of positive and negative happenings might include things like having the right equipment or an interesting lesson, as well as child-centred reasons.

Section Three

Frequency count of disruptive behaviour

Type of behaviour	9.00-10.30	10.45-12.15	1.15-2.15	2.25-3.30
Talking during work time				
Calling out				
Swearing				
Lack of punctuality				
Inattentiveness (e.g. to instructions)				
Untidiness of tables, etc.				
Hitting, pushing, punching, etc.				
Victimisation of particular child				
Spoiling other children's work				
Abuse of equipment				
Deliberate non-compliance				
Rudeness to teacher				
Other — (please specify)				

Instances of annoying behaviour you observe today which happen outside the classroom

Place a stroke in the pertinent column for each instance you observe

Nature of behaviour	Place in school where observed							
	Through corridors	School yard	Lockers	To & from school	Canteen	Toilets	Yard during classtime	Bus areas	Waiting outside classrooms
Physical — bullying, pushing, fighting									
Verbal abuse									
Discourtesy to others/staff									
Discourtesy to others/pupils									
Vandalism									
Theft									
Swearing									
Disregard for others' property									
Trespassing in areas out of bounds									
Smoking									
Littering									

Positive School Discipline: A practical guide to developing policy

Section Three

Instructions

The discipline policy for Chelsea Heights Primary School states that the school aims:
- at creating a caring and concerned attitude throughout the school community;
- to provide a pleasant, stimulating environment for our children;
- to promote in our pupils the ability and disposition to co-operate with others and an awareness and tolerance of other ways of thinking and behaving . . . a sense of identity, achievement and worth.

As part of the discipline policy review, each teacher is asked to complete the two attached pages at the end of each day, for this week.

The first section aims to provide information about the positive things which happened during the day. What did you notice which exemplified, for example:

- caring
- co-operation
- students involved in learning
- provision of a pleasant environment
- tolerance
- a sense of self-respect

Don't feel limited by this list; please record anything you think was positive. Think about the whole day: include class time, out-of-class time, playground, etc.

The second section aims to gather information about what events during the week interfered with achieving our aims. Each teacher is asked to record at the end of each day things which were disruptive. 'Disruptive event' is defined as 'something which interferes with the teaching process and/or the rights of others; e.g. to be safe, to participate'. (Note that in this sense you may view curriculum issues as disruptive.) Think about the whole day: include class time, out-of-class time, playground, etc.

Section Three

Disruptions

A disruption is defined as some event which interferes with the teaching process and/or seriously upsets the normal running of the school and/or rights of others.

Name of teacher:	Day	Time of day
Description of incident	Rating of degree of severity of incident mildly serious serious very serious	
Location (be specific if outside)	If in class, type of lesson and activity involved	Approximate length of time the incident took
Names of student/s others involved		
Brief description of action taken by teacher/others		

Positives

A positive is defined as something which contributes to, or denotes the occurrence of, learning in the student or others; also something which contributes to the caring atmosphere of the school.

Name of teacher:	Day	Time of day
Description of event	Approximate length of time event took	
Location (be specific if outside)	If in class, type of lesson and activity involved	
Names of student/s others involved		
Brief description of action taken by teacher/others		

Positive School Discipline: A practical guide to developing policy

Note that this approach gives information about total school functioning and can be used to answer such questions as the following:
- Are any specific classes particularly disruptive?
- Is there a pattern to disruptions/positives (for example, a high number of incidents on Friday afternoons)?
- Are there any groups of students who are getting more than their share of attention?
- Are there any areas of the curriculum which are noticeably successful in gaining students' interest, or are there specific 'trouble spots'?

The model on which this approach is based can be found in Lawrence, Steed and Young (1983). Schools considering using this idea need to be aware that it will be successful only to the degree that members of the school community are committed to completing the observation sheets.

Interviews

Forget visions of super-smooth TV comperes or nerve-wracking job application interviews. The dictionary says interviews are 'conversations with or questioning of a person' — something we all can do.

Some points to remember:
1. People will be more likely to state their real feelings if they are feeling comfortable, so give some thought to:
   - location (perhaps parents might feel more relaxed at home than at school);
   - setting up chairs side by side rather than having a desk between people;
   - having tea and coffee available.
2. The purpose of the interview needs to be clear to all parties, as does how their responses will be used. Confidentiality may need to be guaranteed.
3. If the interview is to be part of a survey, questions should be worked out and trialled beforehand. In this way comparable information can be gathered by a group of people. Experience will soon show the sort of questions that are most valuable for your purpose. For gauging a range of opinions, open-ended questions are generally the most valuable.

For example:
- What is your view of the present school rules?
- How do you think students should behave in class?
- In your opinion, what responsibilities should pupils in Year 11 take for their study?

The ambush interview

'Bandits' armed with a tape recorder are allowed to stop people briefly during the school day and confront them with a microphone and a question. Well-thought-out questions — 'What is your opinion of teachers' being allowed to smoke in classrooms when students may not?' — can lead to insightful and hilarious, spontaneous comment.

Inter-school visits

Visiting another school can provide stimulating new ideas, information and printed material. It may also give confidence that an approach being used in one's own school is successful elsewhere and endorse a feeling that the home school has something to offer others.

However, in order to be positive, it must be planned carefully so that:
- the aims are clearly specified beforehand;
- those chosen to go can report back to colleagues objectively;
- those staff members chosen to go are prepared to recompense others who took over their usual responsibilities.

Meeting a group of people rather than an individual can also enhance the usefulness of the occasion.

Organisers of such inter-school visits should be aware of possible negative consequences if the school visited is seen as so unlike the home school as to make transfer of ideas and innovations impracticable. ('It's all very well for them but it would never work in our school'.)

Gathering information from students

Even very young children have clear ideas about how they are expected to behave and how others should behave. The youth of the students should not prevent their views and understandings being taken into account. Once children can read and write you will be able to utilise these skills in finding out what they think. The advantage of this technique is the likelihood of gaining a wide range of opinions, especially if you don't ask for names to be put on papers.

Writing
Here are some ideas you might like to use:
- Ask students to answer a single question, for example: 'What school rules do you know?'
- Ask students to write an essay: 'My ideal school', 'A school that is a student's dream', 'A fly on the wall of this classroom (corridor, playground) would see children (or teachers)...'
- Ask them to complete sentences: 'School could be better if...'

In this procedure students should be given as much time as they need, be assured their answers will be confidential, and be told that spelling mistakes will not matter. The teacher could collate the results, copy them and circulate them to interested groups and/or report on them to a staff meeting.

If you use this idea don't ask students a negative question ('What's wrong with this school?') unless you want to feel thoroughly depressed. For some reason the bad things are easier to write about than the good.

Discussions
Interviews can be conducted in a friendly atmosphere with individuals or with small groups of children. (Sometimes senior students can be taught how to do this.) Small-group discussions about topics such as: 'How should you behave in school?' or 'What should happen if you do not do what you are told?' can yield useful information to the inquirer. Discussions in a larger group, although still possibly of value, tend to leave out the ideas of the quieter student. *(See 'Classroom meetings' in the next section for further ideas about these.)*

Positive School Discipline: A practical guide to developing policy 75

Section Three

Taping discussions

To ensure that all the ideas presented in a discussion are recorded, a tape may be made of the proceedings. From this, points may be summarised, and valuable quotes written down; for example:

- 'Teachers tell the tough kids off but give them a second and third chance — don't really do anything about it.'
- 'Mum would get mad if she found out I was in trouble.'
- 'Sometimes you feel like kicking the teacher.'

Section 4:
Meetings and group discussions

In order for as many people as possible to contribute to the process of developing your discipline policy, opportunities must be provided for groups of people to get together and discuss the issues within a structured framework.

The structures for discussions described here will certainly help in gathering information about opinions but, more than that, they can be a valuable means of solving problems, and the techniques learned can actually become part of the ongoing process of policy making, implementation and evaluation.

Group discussions

Group discussions are a good way of gathering information from a relatively large number of people in a short time. The group discussion technique is particularly useful with students provided that they feel safe enough to express their real views. The discussion needs to be carefully planned, both in terms of the topic and its dimensions, and in terms of the other arrangements such as the numbers of people attending, selection of leader/s, briefing of leaders, selection of recorders, time limits, room and seating (arranging the chairs in a circle often facilitates discussion).

The questions asked by the group leader should be open-ended to encourage participants to express their views. The leader might ask:
- 'Do you have anything to add to that, Bill?'
- 'Is that your understanding of the situation, Jane?'
- 'What has been your experience, Mary?'
- 'Others may have a different point of view — what do you think, Paul?'

The size of the group is crucial. It may be that breaking up a large group into smaller groups will permit wider participation in the discussions. This would mean, of course, that more than one leader would need to be appointed. The leader needs to be very clear about the topic for discussion so that interesting but irrelevant tangents can be cut short.

Someone other than the group leader should take notes during the discussion; do not try to rely on memory afterwards. The recorder should be careful to preserve the anonymity of contributors, particularly in the case of students. If participants feel that there may be subsequent recriminations for comments they make, valid information is all the more difficult to obtain.

Two groups of people may need special handling during the meetings — those who want to dominate the topic, and those who wish to comment but lack the assertiveness or confidence to put their view forward. Whether these participants are handled well or not will depend on the skills of the group leader and the technique used (see 'The nominal group technique', in this section.)

Similarly, if conflict arises between two or more participants it is the role of the group leader to intervene with the aim of cooling the conflict while not 'putting down' any of the contributors.

A discussion leader needs the skills to encourage everybody to talk, to keep the comments on the topic and to remain emotionally uninvolved. This is not easy to do. It is imperative therefore to select a leader not on the basis of whether that person is a parent or a teacher but for his or her skills in running this type of meeting. Many schools ask an outsider to lead sensitive discussions.

Classroom meetings

A classroom meeting is a carefully structured discussion in a climate of caring and acceptance where students will feel free to think and express their ideas. These meetings can be held with primary or post-primary students.

Running classroom meetings is by no means a new idea but often such discussions have been subject related. William Glasser (1969) suggests that these discussions can be used to focus on topical school issues, such as discipline, and offers some practical ideas about how to get the most out of such discussions. Glasser describes three distinct types of classroom meetings: open-ended meetings, problem-solving meetings and educational-diagnostic meetings. The first two are particularly relevant in the area of discipline.

Open-ended meetings

Open-ended meetings resemble traditional classroom discussion. In these meetings the teacher presents age-appropriate topics that will intellectually challenge the class. Open-ended meetings are a forum in which good communication skills can be practised and developed. The complementary aims are to encourage understanding and tolerance when listening as well as thoughtfulness and confidence in expression.

Problem-solving meetings

The problem-solving discussion is a meeting in which the class and teacher deal with difficulties that arise in the classroom and school generally. A class might be asked to identify concerns about discipline in the school and then move on to considering ways of improving school discipline. Another topic might be to evaluate or establish school rules and consequences.

How to get started

Attempting to run a classroom meeting without a certain amount of preparation and forethought leads to failure and disillusionment; so does launching oneself without a lot of experience into an important problem-solving discussion with a difficult class. It makes sense to gain experience with reasonably co-operative students — even with small groups, if it can be arranged — and to practise by running as many open-ended meetings as possible. An excellent approach is to work with a more experienced teacher as a leader.

Group management

The physical arrangement of the group is important — a circle is best. All participants can see each other and the communication flow is freer. A sense of equality is fostered because the teacher, although still a leader, is not in a dominant authoritarian position. A circle of chairs is ideal but even if a quick rearrangement of desks is necessary it is worth the effort. In very large classes an inner-outer circle arrangement may be required.

It is important to accept opinions

It is essential that class members learn to abide by a reasonable set of discussion rules. These should consist of only three or four to begin with, but the group might decide to add to these as problems arise. A typical set of rules might be:
- Only one person to talk at a time
- Raise hands to contribute after each speaker has finished
- Show respect to the others by listening carefully
- No put-downs of anyone present or absent

The teacher's approach

In discussing the rules the teacher should make it clear that he or she is going to be consistent and firm in applying them. However, beyond the task of controlling the group, the teacher's leadership manner is the key to the success or failure of the discussion. Knowing and using each student's first name is essential, particularly at the secondary level where seeing large numbers of students for brief periods can sometimes cause a problem. The students should come to see — from the teacher's warmth, enthusiasm and acceptance of their ideas — that the teacher really cares about listening to them. It is important to accept opinions even though there may be private disagreement. A valuable technique that aids this process is to repeat to the speaker and the group, in your own words, what you have understood the speaker to have said.
- 'I reckon that we should only come to school for nine days a fortnight — like my Dad works.'
- 'So you think that kids shouldn't have to spend so much time in school, Jane,' or
- 'It sounds as though you might be finding school a bit boring at times, Jane.'

The frequent use of such reflective

listening, including the reflection of feelings that the teacher perceives as underlying the student's statements, encourages them towards deeper exploration of their ideas. Responses such as those present to the class a model of good communication skills. Students can occasionally be encouraged, as a listening and clarification exercise, to reflect the statements of others before expressing their own thoughts.

Emotions are inevitably generated in classroom meetings and, as teachers are aware, these feelings will mainly be communicated through non-verbal expression, eye contact and posture rather than through the actual language used. By checking their own non-verbal behaviour and by refusing to over-react to the non-verbal messages received from individual students, teachers can gain a great deal of subtle control.

Warm-up activities

Few classes are immediately ready to start discussion without some kind of warm-up activity. These activities can be quite brief, taking only a few minutes, such as having a number of students complete the same unfinished sentence. 'Reading makes me . . .', 'I like . . .', 'Sometimes my mother . . .'. A range of warm-up activities can be found in *100 Ways to Enhance Self Concept in the Classroom* (Canfield and Wells, 1976) or *The Other Side of the Report Card*, (Chase, 1975).

A framework for discussion

If a series of questions (some of which may not be needed if the discussion is proceeding well) is planned before the topic is presented, it will be easier for the teacher to maintain the direction of the class and to stimulate thinking about the topic. Teachers might find the following sequence a useful way to develop a discussion.

Level 1: Defining

Define the topic by asking the students what they think it means. Further questions may be used to explore related aspects of their topic definitions, so that a general consensus can be reached about their understanding of the topic.

Level 2: Personalising

Personalise the topic by relating it to the student's own world. Design questions that draw out his or her own experience and knowledge of the subject.

Level 3: Challenging

At this level of the discussion the teacher's task is to challenge the class to explore the topic in depth. There are many ways of doing this, apart from framing the topic in an unusual way, as already mentioned. Probing, 'What if' questions force the students to think actively and often lead to creative suggestions. The teacher can aid the discussion by linking related ideas and leading the group towards generalisations and positive new applications of these. The teacher should restrain the impulse to supply answers and solutions, a habit that is certain to stifle the group's thinking and expression.

An appropriate role is that of 'devil's advocate', questioning opinions and everyday assumptions. Helping to clarify ideas and summarising points raised in the discussion are also important tasks.

Varying procedures

A planned approach to discussion is a valuable strategy but if the teacher sticks too rigidly to this he or she is in danger of missing the opportunities presented when a student moves the discussion in a creative direction. The plan should be seen as a tentative framework rather than a prescription for outlining the teacher's own ideas.

Occasionally the class can be broken into sub-groups to allow intense discussion of a topic by all class members. The class then reforms to share ideas.

For instance, sub-groups of students could be given a list of questions at the personalising level and leaders appointed to report back some of the ideas to the whole class. An alternative approach is to have sub-group leaders conduct a structured brainstorming session at, say, the definition level of the topic. After a thinking period of a few minutes, during which students individually jot down ideas, the leader collects from each student one or two of his or her best suggestions, perhaps recording them on a large sheet of paper which is passed around the sub-group. These ideas are then presented to the class. Careful instructions need to be given for brainstorming sessions, whether carried out in sub-groups or with the whole class, to avoid premature criticism of ideas, which will stifle creativity and expression.

Winding up

A useful way to wind up the discussion is to get one or two students to summarise the main points. These students may be elected for this task before the discussion begins.

Sometimes discussion in a class does not get going; some children may be restless or uninterested. If many students seem restless it might be better to close the meeting at that point and timetable a further discussion later. Glasser himself readily admits his own failures in many sessions and stresses that only after considerable experience did he gain proficiency and confidence. The potential benefits are these: a deeper sense of belonging, enhanced self-esteem, more involvement in class, and the feeling of strength that comes from having had a say in decisions. These can flow to teachers and students alike.

Brainstorming

This can be a very useful activity to demonstrate the range of options open to the school and the amount of collective knowledge the group has.

Procedure:

The leader says that the group is going to brainstorm possible solutions to a question and explains that:
- The aim is to get as many ideas as possible.
- Solutions offered do not necessarily have to be practical at the moment.
- There will be no initial discussion as to the value of any of the ideas.

The leader presents questions, for example:
- How can we get parents to come to the school?
- What can we do about students who truant?

Answers are recorded on a board or a very large sheet of paper. Following a brainstorming session one or more of the ideas can be taken up for further discussion. Such a discussion might focus on specific ways an idea might be put into practice.

Here is the list that evolved from a five-minute brainstorming session of parents and teachers on the topic, 'Strategies for involving parents':

- Let parents know that teachers will take professional responsibility
- Have a drink with them
- Deliberately include contentious issues
- Cassette recording of a message from the Principal
- 'Telephone tree' for making contact
- More personally addressed letters/invitations etc.
- Home visits
- Family barbecue
- Parents' drop-in room
- Newsletter — list jobs that parents can help with
- Opportunities to see their children do something at school
- Election of parents for each class to perform a liaison role
- Parent involvement in elective schemes
- Parent co-ordinator schemes

Section Four

- Parent resource file
- Joint awareness of 'care role' (parents and teachers)
- Helping with excursions
- Assisting with sport
- Canteen

Force-field analysis

When a school has a problem it is possible using force-field analysis to identify what forces are keeping it from achieving its goals (restraining or blocking forces) and what forces are helping movement towards the goal, (facilitating or driving forces). Using force-field analysis a school can then determine what courses of action will help decrease the strength of the restraining forces and increase the strength of facilitating forces. The choice of action will depend on what means are most practical and what means are in tune with school community values. Action can be implemented and evaluated. If the action doesn't produce results the school chooses other means by the same process until it reaches its goal (or sees that the goal is impossible!) Two useful references on force-field analysis are Blachford (1984) and Spier in Pfeiffer and Jones's Handbook (1973); both are listed in Part Three.

Force-field analysis can be used at other levels too, to analyse problems within particular groups of students or to assist individuals who are experiencing problems.

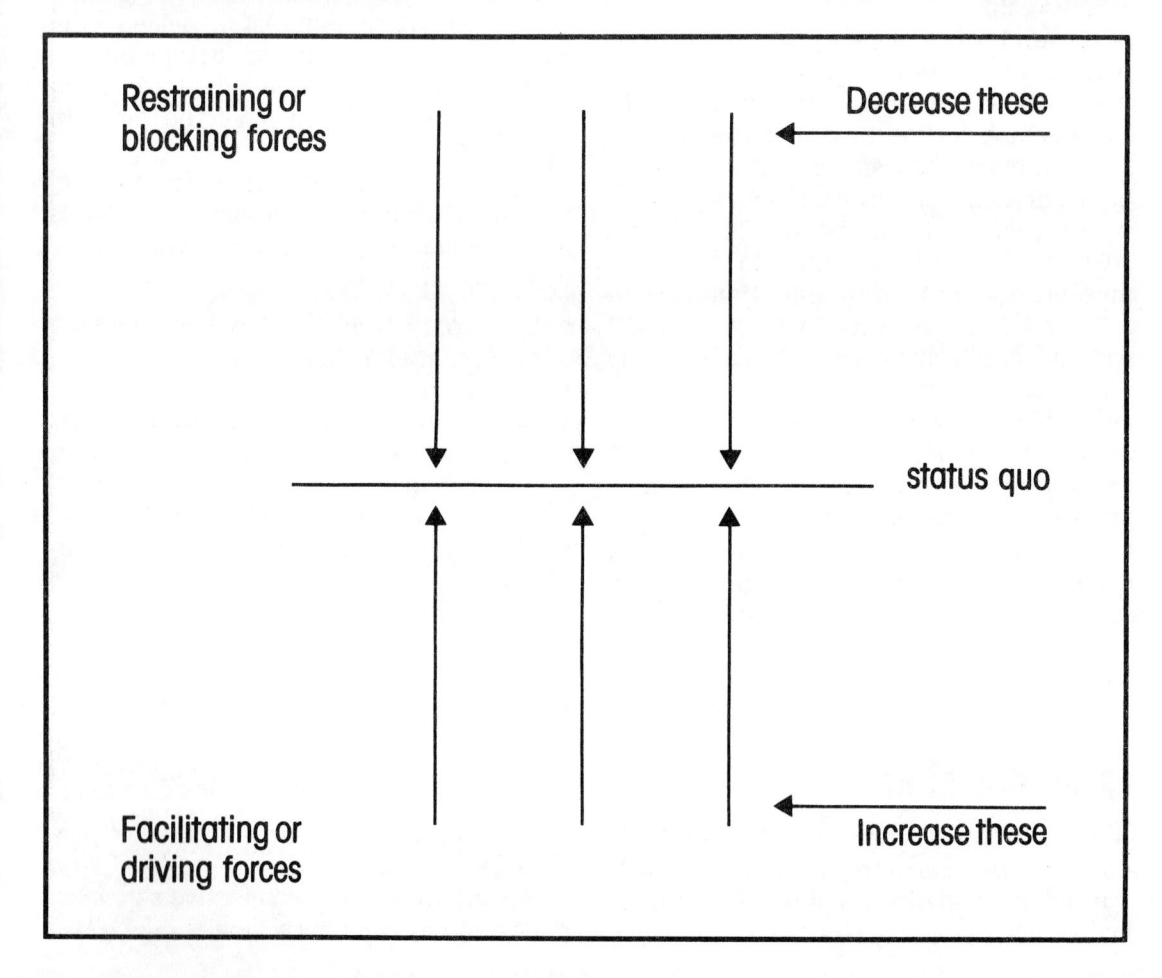

Restraining or blocking forces ← Decrease these

———————————— status quo

Facilitating or driving forces ← Increase these

82 Positive School Discipline: A practical guide to developing policy

Section Four

Analysis sheets

1. Group statement of the problem. (Be very specific.)

2. Blocking forces: What are some of the factors that keep the problem a problem?

Driving forces: What are some of the driving forces which could help solve the problem?

3. Review your list of blocking forces and underline those forces which you think you might be able to modify, in step 4.

Section Four

4. Identified blocking forces   Possible action steps to reduce
                                      effect of blocking force*

A

B

C

D

Consider each underlined blocking force and brainstorm action steps that you could take to reduce or eliminate the force.
(*Change is often more easily effected by reducing blocking forces than by increasing driving forces.)

5. Review action steps and underline the three or four most practical.

6. Action steps (From 5)
Resources: Available   Required

7. Select most favoured action step which will help to reduce the effect of an influential blocking force.

Nominal group technique

The nominal group technique is a structured process that can be used by groups in reviewing, planning or fact-finding tasks. The process assists a group to work together efficiently to identify priorities and is designed to get everyone contributing ideas. Four conditions are essential to the successful and satisfying use of this process:

- The question or task to be addressed is clearly defined.
- A skilled group facilitator is available.
- Large groups are divided into smaller sub-groups of from five to eight.
- Two hours of uninterrupted time are available.

Be clear about the objective of the meeting. Decide what is the most useful question to meet your objective. Defining the task or question clearly is essential.

For example: 'What strategies or procedures can our staff adopt to improve the management of student behaviour at our school?'

Setting the scene

Seat the groups in semi-circles around a board or large sheet of paper. Provide felt pens or chalk and pencils and paper. Pre-arrange groups, nominating a leader and a scribe for each small group. Brief small-group leaders prior to the session.

Procedure

The facilitator welcomes the whole group, outlines the task, and summarises the nominal group process. Participants move to pre-arranged small groups. The small-group leader's role is to guide participants through the following steps, to act as a timekeeper and to participate.

Step 1: Silent generation of ideas in writing (10 minutes)
- Without discussion, individuals list in brief phrases their responses to the task question as outlined in the introduction.

Step 2: Round-robin recording of ideas (15 minutes)
- Each participant presents (in round-robin fashion) one idea from his or her personal list. Record this on board or large sheet of paper. Round-robin continues until all ideas are listed. Participants may 'pass', or re-enter when their turn comes. Ideas should not be discussed at this point.

Step 3: Discussion of ideas for clarification (15 minutes)
- Leader takes group through each item to check that the meaning is clear. Participants can either ask for clarification or make a brief statement of why the idea is important. As final preferences will be expressed in voting, choices need not be made. If items are duplicated, contributors must agree before the items are collapsed to one. Give each item an alphabetical letter at the end of this stage.

Step 4: Voting and setting priorities (10 minutes)
- Each group member selects the five items he or she considers most important and ranks them on five separate voting slips as follows:

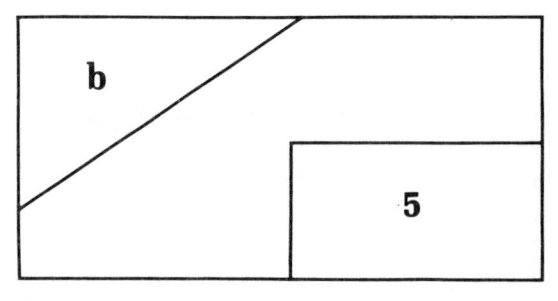

```
+-----------------------+
|          /            |
|   b     /             |
|        /---------+    |
|       /          |    |
|      /     5     |    |
|                  |    |
+------------------+----+
```

Ranking:
5 = most important
4 = next in importance, and so on.

Voting slips are collected by a group member for tallying. The five items found to be most highly ranked should be written on the board or large sheets of paper for display to the whole group.

Step 5: Use this step, if a number of small

groups are involved, to get a final set of five priorities.
- Small groups display priorities to whole group. Items from all groups are given in alphabetical order, meaning is clarified through brief discussion and, where agreed, some items may be collapsed together. All participants vote again as in Step 4 and the final votes are tallied.

Note: The same process can be used to identify solutions and resources to meet priorities.

Policy improvement planning sheet

The policy improvement planning sheet provides another structured framework for identifying concerns and generating solutions. It can be used by an individual or a group. The steps provide a means of keeping thinking or discussion 'on the track'.

Policy improvement planning sheet

Workshop

1. **Problems**
   1. ....
   2. ....
   3. ....
   4. ....
   5. ....
   6. ....

2. **Problem to be worked on**

   ....
   ....
   ....
   ....

3. **Goal: (Positive restatement of problem)**

   ....
   ....
   ....

4. **Strategies to achieve goal — brainstorm possibilities**
   Asterisk those strategies which seem realistic.

   ....
   ....
   ....
   ....

5. **Steps required to implement strategies**
   For each strategy you think has promise work out steps, persons responsible, resources needed, review date, and success indicators.

   Strategy: ....
   ....

	Who will be responsible?	What resources will be needed?	When will we review?	How will we know if strategy is successful?
Strategy 1. .... Steps				
Strategy 2. .... Steps				

Positive School Discipline: A practical guide to developing policy

Section Four

The completed policy improvement planning sheet might look something like this:

1. **Problem indicators**

   Excessive noise in classrooms; learning disrupted; in-school suspension over-used; in-school suspension not used when appropriate.

2. **Identified problem/issue**

   Teachers experiencing difficulty with classroom management.

3. **Goal**

   To provide opportunities for specific teachers to develop/implement appropriate classroom management skills and/or minimise the negative impact of specific teachers.

4. **Strategies**
   - Develop a clearly specified disciplinary policy and procedure as a resource for all teachers.
   - Generally stress communal concern, corporate responsibility in all discussion and written policy on discipline.
   - Incorporate expectation into policy that co-ordinators will assist teachers in negotiating and working through problems with students where classroom conflict has occurred.
   - Co-ordinators, and/or heads of department use accepted school discipline policy and procedures as basis for discussion with individual teachers about what is going on in the classroom. Aim to keep discussion at a professional level.
   - Train co-ordinators to use a structured problem-solving approach in talking to teachers experiencing difficulty and to keep discussion on a constructive level (for example, Thomas Gordon's No-Lose Method, or William Glasser's Reality Therapy problem-solving approach).
   - Enlist help of support services to work in classroom with teacher.
   - Provide skills training (for example, Systematic Training for Effective Teaching, Teacher Effectiveness Training) for invited groups inside school.

- Encourage teachers to attend external, relevant in-service courses. Create environment wherein it is accepted that teachers sit in on each other's classes; experienced teachers to model this by inviting others into their classes and also by moving into classes themselves to learn.
- Encourage team teaching, joint responsibility.
- Encourage teachers to audiotape own lessons for self-evaluation and/or sharing with other staff, encourage use of the 'clinical supervision' model where peers are invited to assist with observation and feedback.
- Provide stress-reduction information to staff.
- Co-ordinator initiates entry to classes to observe particular students and use an objective observation checklist. This material can be used as the basis for discussion of student behaviour and alternative teacher responses.
- A direct approach from someone in a position of responsibility — head of department/subject co-ordinator/level co-ordinator or principal — may be necessary. Problem should not be left to worsen without intervention.

5. **To be worked on**

Select usable strategies from the above list. For each strategy work out steps, person responsible, resources needed, review or completion date.

Modified community conference technique

The technique described here has been adapted from 'The Community Conference Technique' in *The School Policy Manual*, by Andrews, Bryant and Pankhurst (1981) *(see References for availability.)*

The community conference technique can help achieve two main aims:
- to give everybody an opportunity to have their say on a particular topic, and
- to get an idea of how participants rate the various suggestions.

Method

1. Invitations are issued, perhaps in several languages, to discuss the topic; for example, 'How do you think students should behave in school?'

2. The conference room is set up prior to the meeting with tables and chairs in small groups. Very large sheets of paper and coloured felt-tip pens will be needed. Tables should be numbered. Interpreters should have been arranged if necessary.

3. After introductions and welcome, groups

Section Four

are told the task. Each group appoints a leader and a recorder.

4. Time is spent brainstorming ideas about the question. All ideas are recorded without comment. Each page has the table number written on it.
5. When people have run out of ideas, each group passes its sheet on to the next table. Each idea is rated by the new group in accordance with the following:
   A. Most important
   B. Important
   C. Worth considering
   D. Only of a little importance
   E. Doesn't matter

   (Note: Give each group a different coloured pen for ease of reading.)

   Groups are allowed, indeed encouraged, to write comments on others' sheets; for example, 'We're not sure what this means' or 'This is okay if you're talking about younger children'.

   If you're using a voting method for deciding your rating, then you should record if some members of the group have strongly disagreed with the majority — and why, if possible.
6. Each of the sheets is rated by one or more groups other than the writers.
7. When the sheet is finally returned to the writing group, they should read the comments of others and their ratings, before evaluating the ideas they originally put forward.
8. At this stage, the sheets can be gathered to be collated and the results subsequently distributed.
9. Alternatively, each group takes small cards and puts just one of their ideas on each card, together with their group number and rating. In the meantime, the organisers, having listened in on the discussions, will have decided on summary headings (for example — co-operation, self-discipline, obedience, respect for others) and will have made cards with these headings on and placed them on a large table. As the groups get their cards filled in, they place these on the large table under the appropriate headings. These card listings are then collated.
10. Participants are thanked and coffee is served.

Factors that can influence the length of time this conference takes are: the number of participants and the degree of debate over the issues. It is important to allow enough time for people to feel they have a chance to be heard and to ensure that the group leaders have the skills to allow this to happen.

Section 5:
In-service education

At various stages in the process of developing a discipline policy, your school community might benefit from some in-service education; for example on the subject of alternative methods of developing self control, or how to manage conflict.

In order for programmes to be successful, several factors need to be considered. Firstly, it is pointless to put valuable time and energy into I.S.E. if a clear need for such a programme does not exist. Secondly, a one-off event is unlikely to achieve a large change, so if change is the aim the in-service activity must be tied in to ongoing programmes of information gathering, reporting back, and decision making within the school.

Thirdly, appropriate steps must be planned within the I.S.E. to ensure that it is an effective learning experience. Joyce and Showers (1980) distinguish between two kinds of I.S.E: one in which the aim is for teachers to improve a skill in their existing repertoire, and one where new skills are taught. Obviously 'fine-tuning' of already acquired skills will be easier than developing new attitudes and theoretical understanding. Joyce and Showers also indicate that adults are excellent learners if the following five conditions for learning are met:

1. New theory must be presented to the school community in such a way that they get a clear understanding of what it's about. Such a presentation on its own, however, is not enough to bring about real change.
2. New skills should be taught through film or modelling procedures so that an example is presented.
3. These skills should be practised in a simulated setting. We all take time to feel comfortable with any new skills, hence we need to practise and to gain insight into our performance.
4. When new skills are practised, feedback is required so that we do not fall into the many traps awaiting us. 'Tricks of the trade' can be picked up at this stage.
5. Finally, it seems that teachers and other adults can gain much from coaching each other. This may take some courage, but can result in increased confidence and long-term change.

Section five

If you are planning a large change, all of the five steps above must be included. Finally, to ensure a successful I.S.E. programme, sufficient time, energy and commitment from planners and participants are essential.

Planning

This checklist may be useful to you in your planning sessions:
a) Co-ordinator
b) Content
c) Guest speaker
d) Handouts (prior to and during the I.S.E. day)
e) Funding (who will apply?)
f) Location (venues away from school receive positive acclaim!)
g) Refreshments (good lunches rate well!)
h) Equipment
i) Chairperson
j) Evaluation
k) Agenda (does it include an interesting variety of activities?)
l) Name tags
m) Materials (for example, butcher's paper, Textas, and masking tape)
n) Plan of sessions
o) Publicity (see 'Circulars' in Section 1)

You could plan advance publicity, say three weeks beforehand.

Then two weeks beforehand ask participants to respond to a brief questionnaire; for example, 'I think the most important aspect of discipline that needs to be discussed is . . .' These responses must be used for your planning and you will find that this really helps to clarify your objectives. One week beforehand, a 'Welcome to the Curriculum Day' notice with date, time and place could be given to each participant together with a brief article to read.

On the day itself, the organisers should be early to greet participants and arrange tea and coffee. The room should be set up so that participants sit in a circle rather than in a classroom arrangement. Organisers should ensure the timetable is closely kept to. It's awful being the last speaker for the day and finding you are left with only half your allocated time.

Ideas discussed in the Section 1 article, 'Community meetings', and in several Section 4 articles, are also relevant to the planning, conduct and follow-up of an in-service activity.

Do try to blend humour into the day — learning is likely to be greater!

Guest speakers

A guest speaker can be either a godsend or a great mistake. To ensure the former, organisers need to be clear about the contribution the guest speaker is supposed to make. Is the speaker's task to get people interested in the topic, to convey a theory, or to report on a practice? The answer to this question should help you decide whom to choose.

Try to ensure that at least one person in the community has heard the suggested guest speaker, and can vouch for his or her skills.

If you want to arouse interest you will need someone who can raise the appropriate questions and present arguments in a lively (perhaps even provocative) fashion. The information conveyed, in contrast, needs to be able to stick closely to the point. What you don't want is somebody who will turn your audience off or send them to sleep.

Having decided why you want a guest speaker and who it should be, make some notes so that whoever contacts the guest speaker can give him or her a clear brief. If the guest speaker agrees to perform the task at the specified time, confirm all the details in writing.

A few days before the big event, ring the guest speaker to assure him or her of a welcome — this also serves as a reminder. Ask if any audio/visual equipment will be required.

After it's all over, a 'thank you' in writing is usually appreciated, especially if it mentions the particularly useful aspects of the presentation.

Films and videos

Films and videos can be great to arouse interest, give information or provide food for thought and discussion.

It is a good idea, however, to observe the following precautions:
- Preview the film or video. Don't be misled by a title. *You've got to be flexible* is not a management film — it's about low back pain!
- Ensure that you know the type of projector needed for the film and that you have a trained operator.
- Check both of these things again on the day before the film is due to be shown.
- Be quite clear about the purpose of showing the film and work out beforehand what aspects are to be discussed and how. This means writing down specific questions and perhaps selecting small groups. Consider giving the audience the questions before showing the film.
- Films and videos are often made with a specific audience in mind. Thus a film made for teachers could assume knowledge of educational theory that is not necessarily shared by the parent groups. Showing such a film to parents could be counter-productive unless some good briefing is given beforehand.

Making workshops work

To ensure that people do not sit listening passively hour after hour, many organisers plan structured workshops as part of in-service activities.

Think about the following questions:
- **What are the objectives of the workshop?**

Make a brief list, for example: to give everyone a chance to express a point of view; to have the group reach agreement; to come up with a list of concerns/possibilities.

- **What process will we use in the workshop?**

In this section and in Section 4, several

processes and sample workshops are described. Choose one that will be most likely to help you achieve your desired outcome. This could vary from general discussion, through structured processes like the 'Nominal group technique' to skills-practice or role-play. The process you choose will determine the number of people you should have in each group.

- **How will the workshop group be formed?**

It's best to arrange your groupings prior to the day so that attention can be given to getting the right mix of people to work together. Lists of the groups and locations can be displayed on the day.

- **Who will lead the workshop groups?**

You will need to consider which members of the school community might be prepared and able to lead the workshop (that is, to keep it on track). However group leaders are selected, the quality of the workshop sessions will be improved if you hold a briefing session for leaders beforehand. For some workshops you will also need to appoint scribes.

- **Where will the groups work?**

Try to allocate enough space or rooms for groups to work without distracting or interrupting each other. The working areas should be close to your main venue so that time is not wasted in moving to and from the workshop groups.

- **How will we conclude the workshop segment of the programme?**

Sometimes it is useful to have a plenary session with small groups reporting back to the whole group or an open plenary session for comments from groups. Be wary of setting up long-winded reporting-back sessions which put everybody to sleep. It may be more constructive to display and/or collate the scribes' records of the workshop instead.

Section five

Sample agenda for workshop: Improving our policy

We need your help to improve the effectiveness of our disciplinary procedures. Today we would like to identify problems with the current system and to get your suggestions for improvements.

Process

1a. Please take five minutes to silently list on the accompanying sheet the problems which you believe do or might stop our current discipline policy from working effectively.

   b. Briefly share your views with other group members. You could do this by going around the circle with each person giving one idea in turn, then repeating the process until all ideas have been shared.

2. Choose one problem to work on. You could vote here to see which problem your group wants to give priority to.

3. Start working on the problem by restating it as a goal — that is, the positive change you want to achieve.

4. Brainstorm strategies which might assist in achieving the goal. Don't evaluate the strategies at this point; just list as many as possible. You can choose the best strategies in the next step.

5. Select one or two realistic and promising strategies and work out how they might be put into action.

In-service or community meeting planning sheet

We have found it useful to prepare planning sheets so that people know who has responsibility for what. It also helps to avoid serious omissions, such as who is going to arrange the projector for the film on which the whole day is based. An example of a planning sheet follows.

The following pages show how such a form can be used to help you plan in-services or other meetings. Tasks to be done on the day or beforehand are indicated and responsibilities allocated under the headings shown. All members of the planning group need to have a copy of the plan.

Notice that details of the session content and purpose (other vital aspects of planning a successful day) are shown in the programme that follows.

Section five

Time	Title of session	Format	Tasks on the day and people doing them	Handouts, materials, equipment	Things to be done beforehand and by whom
8.45 (am)	Coffee and Registration		– Set up rooms – Welcoming committee – Collect lunch money (Jo, Bill, Jenny)	– Name tags – Programme – Tea, coffee and accessories	– Contact lunch caterers (Bill) – Choose small discussion groups and write name tags with label on each (Jo) – Collect urn, tea, coffee biscuits etc. (Bill) – Flowers for room (Jenny) – Programme and all other handouts (Jo)
			Chairperson (am): John Smith		
9.00	Welcome and Introduction	Whole group	– Welcome (John S) – Introduction (Liz)	– Overhead projector, pens and transparencies	– Confirm and discuss briefly with John and Liz (Jenny) – Collect overhead etc. (Bill)
9.30	Workshop. How do we want our students to behave?	Small groups	– Introduce task and conduct plenary (Liz) – Groups to nominate their own leader and scribe	– Butcher's paper, felt pens	– Collect butcher's paper and pens (Jo)
10.30	Coffee		– Check coffee supplies (Bill) – Confirm lunch arrangements (Bill)		
11.00	How do we achieve our goals: approaches to behaviour management	Whole group	– Speaker (Ray) – Role-play (Jo and Bill) – Announce lunch arrangements (Bill)	– Overhead etc. – Handouts – Wolfgang and Glickman – Beliefs inventory – Glasser's Eight Steps – School and Discipline	– Confirm and brief Ray (Jenny)

Section five

Chairperson (pm): Jo

Time	Activity	Format		
1.15	Developing a Behaviour Management Programme	Whole group	– Speaker (Liz) – Film ("Ten Steps")	– Projector (Jenny) – Film (Liz)
2.15	Workshop. The steps we will take to manage classroom behaviour problems—preventive and problem solving	Small groups	– Introduction and plenary (Liz) – Worksheets for small groups	– Prepare worksheets and evaluation form (Jo, Bill, Jenny and Liz)
3.00	Plenary			

3.20	Evaluation			– Other things to do
				– Book hall (Bill)
				– Publicity: (Bill, Jo)
				  – circulars
				  – invitation/accept forms
				  – letters
				  – talk to staff (Bill)
				  – talk to council (Jo, Bill, Jenny)

Positive School Discipline: A practical guide to developing policy

Section five

Sample programme for a primary school in-service
Developing a school-based discipline policy

Objectives — to be used in introducing the in-service programme:
1. to present the stages schools go through in developing a discipline policy;
2. to identify the goals of this school's discipline policy in terms of desired behaviours to be expected from students/teachers/parents;
3. to provide an overview of some common approaches to behaviour management;
4. to begin to identify preventive and problem-solving steps this school could adopt as part of its discipline policy;
5. to clarify areas which will need further attention following the in-service and to allocate responsibilities for follow-through.

8.45   Coffee
9.00   Introduction

Purpose: to provide a context for the in-service in terms of statewide developments, social trends and the school's particular needs.

Content:
- Societal changes
- Changes to Education Department Regulations, the abolition of corporal punishment and the need for schools to develop discipline policies
- Value of whole-school approach and parental involvement
- Stages schools go through in developing a discipline policy (What stage has this school reached?)
- Feedback on staff survey on discipline
- Programme and objectives for today

9.30   Workshop: 'How do we want our students to behave?'

Purpose: to provide an opportunity for members of the school community to reach some agreement on what behaviours the school wishes to promote. (Start at the beginning: What are our goals?)

Format: group discussion. Nominate leader and recorder. Use 'Describing school behaviour' exercise (see Section 2.) Could

extend to the behaviour we want from parents and teachers too!
   Use results as basis for school rules or code of behaviour (following I.S.E. day).

10.30   Morning tea

11.00   How do we achieve our goals?: Approaches to behaviour management.
   Purpose: to provide a brief overview of useful behaviour management strategies from a variety of theories.
   Content:
- Introduce concepts of preventive and problem-solving strategies.
- Introduce Wolfgang and Glickman's 'Teacher Behaviour Continuum' and the view that teachers need a variety of strategies in their repertoire.
- Give 'Beliefs about Discipline Inventory' from Wolfgang and Glickman (1981).
- Introduce some key concepts from three major approaches:
   Behaviour modification: reinforcement to promote desirable behaviour, rather than punishment; individual and group approaches.
   Individual psychology (Dreikurs/Adler): goals of behaviour and logical consequences.
   Reality Therapy (Glasser): "Schools without Failure" philosophy and the Reality Therapy problem-solving approach.
   Demonstrate, using teacher-student script to illustrate a good problem-solving discussion with a student.
   Discuss strengths and limitations.

1.15 Developing a behaviour management programme for our school
   Purpose: to present one approach to managing disruptive behaviour (with both preventive and problem-solving elements) as a basis for the school to start developing its own approach.
   Format:
- Introduce Glasser's ten steps to discipline in the context of the Reality Therapy concepts presented before lunch.
- View "Ten Steps" film and discuss strengths and limitations of the approach.

2.15   Workshop
The steps we will take to manage classroom behaviour problems (preventive and problem-solving approaches):
- Prepare a structured worksheet for this workshop (groups of 6-8 plus leader and recorder).

3.00   Plenary — Where to from here?
- What areas should our discipline policy cover?
- What do we still need to work on and how will we go about it? For example: rules/code; getting more parent and student involvement; procedures for handling confrontations; positive programmes to reduce misbehaviour;
- Set some goals and plan action; and nominate a group to co-ordinate follow-through.

3.20   Evaluation
1. What I found most useful . . .
2. What I found least useful . . .
3. What I want more of . . .

Sample programme for a post-primary in-service

Background: This programme was prepared in response to staff interests and needs as expressed in a survey conducted by the school's welfare committee. The request to Student Services was made through the school's regular Student Services officer. The welfare committee accepted responsibility for practical organisation of the day.

The overall aims of the programme were:
1. to consider existing management strategies in the school;
2. to introduce some new approaches;
3. to place the issue of school discipline in the context of school organisation;
4. to obtain recommendations for action on school policy.

Preparation: Prior to the I.S.E. day all staff were asked to complete a questionnaire to evaluate their disciplinary techniques to establish a 'mental set' for the day.

Programme

9.15   Introduction: School organisation and structures — their relationship to discipline

9.45   Activity: Memories of school (see Section 2)
   Goals:
1. to break the ice and get participants actively involved in the programme;
2. to draw conclusions from teachers' own school experiences which could provide a basis for evaluating current practices at the school.

10.15   Taped survey: How the students view the school, teachers and discipline
   Goal: To give teachers feedback on student perspective to complement their own views (past and present)
   Strategy: Prior to the in-service, the outside consultant interviewed representative groups of students in Years 7-9. During the session some of their taped comments were played and key comments were summarised on overhead transparencies.

10.30   Morning tea

10.50   Talk and activity: Three models of discipline
   Goal: To provide an overview of current classroom management models
   Strategy: Talk based on McDaniel article, 'Exploring alternatives to punishment — the keys to effective discipline' (1980). Brief activity on emphasising the positive. Each teacher asked to correct a maths sheet in a way he/she would consider most productive. Methods shared and discussed with positive model recommended.

11.30   Small-group task (1): Positive strategies
   Goal: To provide a forum for discussion of positive strategies which could be used within the school to promote positive behaviour
   Strategy: Small groups with recorders arranged prior to session. Small groups discuss and record ideas in the following areas:
   a) positive strategies to be used in the classroom;
   b) positive strategies to be used to improve relationships between home and school;

Section five

c) positive strategies to improve outside class behaviour.
Recorders present key ideas for summary to plenary session.

12.00 Lunch

1.15 Talk and activity: Punishment
   Goal: To define punishment and look at its role in school discipline
   Strategy: Talk on punishment and logical consequences. Small-group task (2):
a) Questions on punishment:
- Why do you use punishment?
- What does punishment do?
- List some effective punishments
- List some ineffective punishments

b) Find logical consequences for the following behaviours:
- Unfinished classroom assignments
- Pushing or shoving in line
- Vandalism
- Fighting at recess or lunchtime
- Running in the corridor

1.45 Video and discussion: Glasser's approach to discipline
   Goal: To present one disciplinary approach to be evaluated by staff in terms of relevance and applicability
   Strategy:
a) Introduction to Glasser's Reality Therapy
b) Film: "Ten Step Discipline Program"
c) Discussion

3.15 Discussion: Towards a discipline policy
   Goal: To draw conclusions and get recommendations from group for future directions
   Strategy: Discussion of alternatives. Possible involvement of consultants.
   Outcome: Welfare Committee to follow up session and report back to Education Committee (whole staff). Meeting of consultants and Welfare Committee arranged to begin work on recommendation.

Section 6:
Working out differences through discussion

Differences are bound to occur throughout the process of creating a discipline policy and then, later, when implementing it. Policy makers, therefore, need to decide on the procedures they will use to resolve conflict now and in the future.

Minor issues often become major problems in schools because of ineffective problem-solving strategies, yet a private interview with a student away from the pressures of the classroom can be a valuable way of working through a conflict. However, certain approaches to conflict resolution quite commonly used in teacher–student interviews are guaranteed to fail. These include both aggressive approaches which rely on interrogation, moralising, and advice-giving, and unassertive approaches which are overly sympathetic or passive. The aggressive and unassertive styles work no better in schools than they do with adults at work. The John Cleese management-training film *'I'd like a word with you — the discipline interview'* illustrates this point. Thomas Gordon (1974) describes these communication styles as 'door-slammers'.

Unfortunately, although good problem-solving skills don't appear to come naturally the ineffective styles do, particularly when we are under stress. The good news is that we can learn communication skills that will help us to become better problem-solvers in discipline interviews. For teachers used to controlling the direction of exchanges in the classroom this learning may involve the breaking of old habits. There is hope for the motivated and open-minded teacher.

Two approaches for use in teacher-student interviews (or other interviews) are provided here as problem-solving frameworks for teachers:
- The No-lose Method of conflict resolution (Thomas Gordon); and
- the eight steps of Reality Therapy (William Glasser).

These approaches appear deceptively easy, but they are highly dependent on the teacher having the skills:
- to attend to verbal and non-verbal behaviour (how people sit, stand, look);
- to listen without prejudging;
- to communicate understanding of feelings and thoughts;

Section Six

- to clarify through exploratory questions;
- to summarise feelings and thoughts;
- to present alternative perspectives and to challenge in a helpful way; and
- to assist in goal setting.

A carefully designed staff-development programme and the assistance of a good resource person could provide teachers with the opportunity to practise these communication skills in a supportive setting. Don't be put off by the initial awkwardness of such practice sessions. It takes time for staff to feel comfortable with such exercises and time for individuals to incorporate these skills into a comfortable blend with their own personal style. The Teacher Effectiveness Trainers suggest a four-stage process of skill acquisition that will be reassuring to beginners:

1. unconsciously unskilled
2. consciously unskilled
3. consciously skilled
4. unconsciously skilled

In addition to the development of skills, two prior conditions are likely to increase a teacher's chances of success in using these methods. Firstly, it is important to work towards establishing a good relationship with individual students. This means using whatever opportunity arises to talk to students in a friendly, nonacademic manner; initiating contact through greetings, a smile, using the students' names; finding out (and remembering) something about the world of students outside school; being on the lookout for areas of interest, talent or strength; encouraging wherever possible. It is particularly important to make an extra effort to do these things with students you find difficult to manage. If you can't catch them 'being good', acknowledge them when they're just 'being bearable'. With a friendly relationship, a student will be more motivated to work things out with you when a conflict arises.

The second and equally important pre-condition is to have a set of rules which clearly specify the behaviours that are acceptable or unacceptable in the classroom. It is a valuable exercise to have students participate in setting class rules and consequences. Students are more likely to be committed to rules they have had some part in making. The rules provide a baseline against which future conflicts may be resolved.

Remember that problem-solving discussion, interviews or conferences with students (or with parents or colleagues) may start at different points depending on the preceding events. Carefully chosen opening statements and good judgement about the direction you take can enhance the likelihood of a constructive outcome.

The No-lose Method of conflict resolution

Thomas Gordon describes this approach to conflict resolution fully in his book *Teacher Effectiveness Training (1974) (see References and Resources)*. The No-lose Method is contrasted with 'win-lose' strategies in which one person (teacher or student) wins at the expense of the other. Although win-lose strategies are common in everyday negotiations they can have some serious disadvantages which limit their effectiveness. For example, the loser may choose either fight or flight. A fighting loser may actively sabotage the solution or seek to re-open the fight; the loser in flight may passively resist accepting the solution or avoid the winner. In both cases the relationship is likely to deteriorate.

The No-lose Method has a number of advantages. It can lead to:

- a greater commitment and motivation to make the plan work;
- no resentment because the solution meets the needs of all parties;
- better solutions because more than one person suggests alternatives;
- greater responsibility on the part of students.

It can be used with one student or a group of students (or with adults). To use the method effectively requires practice and skill in listening openly to other viewpoints and communicating that understanding and the ability to state one's own view of the problem without blaming or denigrating someone else. It can be used by a teacher directly involved in a conflict with a student, or by a third party acting as a mediator.

There are six steps in the No-lose Method. To develop goodwill at the start of negotiations, it can be helpful to outline the steps in the process. It is important that the teacher gives the message, 'I refuse to use my power to win at the expense of your losing, but I also refuse to let you win at the expense of my losing. I want to respect your needs, but I must also repect my own. Let's try a new approach that will help us find a solution that will meet both your needs and mine. The solution we're after is one that allows us both to win.' (Gordon 1974)

Before using this method you would need to decide whether you feel comfortable about entering into a negotiating and collaborative relationship with the student and whether you have the necessary time to spend outside class with the student. Initially it will be up to you to teach the student this approach to problem solving. If you and the student are angry it is best to have a cooling-off period before you meet.

The six steps of the No-lose Method are:
1. Defining the problem
2. Generating possible solutions
3. Evaluating the solutions
4. Making the decisions, choosing solutions
5. Planning how to act on the decision
6. Evaluating the success of the solution

1. Defining the problem

Open the discussion with a statement such as 'We have a problem we need to sort out'. You should start by clearly stating your view of the problem. Pinpoint specifically the behaviour that is causing you concern. 'Messages' which state your unmet need can be useful here; for example, 'I get annoyed when I lose my concentration and have to start things over again'. Avoid stating the problem in terms of your solution, 'I want you to be quiet'. It's also best to avoid blaming, sarcastic or exaggerated statements such as 'You're always calling out in class'. These comments rarely convince the student of the error of his ways and often produce resistance and defensiveness.

Some teachers do not feel comfortable discussing a conflict in terms of their own feelings because they think the student may take advantage of this. We suggest that it is a matter of judgement and confidence. State your feelings assertively to the extent that you feel comfortable. Explain that you cannot accept behaviour that breaks the rules agreed upon by the class.

It is equally important to get the student to state his or her view of the problem. Use open-ended questions to get the student's point of view; for example, 'How do you see the problem, John?' or 'Sally, I've said I don't think things are working out in class at the moment. What do you think is happening?' Don't give in to the all-too-human temptation to ask, 'Why did you do it?' Often the student has no idea why he or she acted in a particular way and 'why' questions develop the habit of excuse making. If the student blames others or talks about past events, acknowledge the statements but bring the focus back to the issues over which you and the student seem to have some control.

To show the student you are trying to understand his or her point of view, even if you don't agree with it, you may restate it in your own words or ask for clarification. You may also comment tentatively on a feeling you sense behind the student's words; for example, 'You seem to be feeling really uptight about the work we're doing'. Checking out has many advantages; in addition to showing the students that you are really trying to understand, it reduces the likelihood of misunderstandings which can arise if we indulge in mind reading. It can also show the students that you can cope with the expression of negative feelings and this will free them to sort out their thoughts and feelings so they will be ready to work on a solution. Sometimes during this process a student may criticise you, directly or indirectly. This won't be comfortable but if your conscience is clear don't fall into the trap of defending yourself. Just acknowledge that you see things differently. If you think the criticism is warranted be ready to acknowledge a mistake you have made and to change, because you'll be expecting the student to do the same. We are all fallible.

2. Generating possible solutions

Brainstorming involves generating as many solutions as possible. You can start the process by asking, 'What ideas do you have about how we can solve this problem? Let's see how many different solutions we can come up with. I'll write them down'. Don't criticise the solutions at this stage; evaluation comes later. By suspending evaluation you can encourage creativity and quantity. If you write down some wild and far-fetched solutions this can provide light relief for you both. Your list of solutions will include ways in which the student could change what he or she is doing to follow the rules better and ways in which you could change your behaviour to help the student do this. For a student (John) who seems to start fights with two other students in class, the list might look like this:

- Move to a different class.
- Sit away from Bill and Fred.
- Sit in front row.
- Count to ten when angry.
- Meet with teacher and Bill and Fred to sort out the problem.
- Teacher tell Bill and Fred off.
- Send Bill and Fred to another class.
- Teacher use private signs to remind John of the rules.

A student is far more likely to abide by the realistic solution that he or she has created than the 'perfect' one that you come up with. Offer a solution as a prompt to the student (referred to from now on as 'he' for the sake of convenience only; we know girls can have problems too) if he's really struggling to get started but otherwise let the student take the lead. If he senses you are not going to jump on his ideas, this will help. Repeat the student's idea so he knows you have registered it. With a very reserved student you may want him to write down his ideas first.

Sometimes it can be helpful to break at this point to allow the student some time to think of other ideas. If you do this, fix a firm time to continue.

3. Evaluating the solutions

Look through the list together and cross out those solutions that are not acceptable to you or to the student. You may have to cross some out because you have no control over the elements in the solution (that is, it relates to wider school or community rules; for example, the student may suggest going home early if he behaves well). Get the student talking about his reactions to each solution. Listen for his feelings so you can determine which solution is likely to work best. State your own feelings clearly; for example, 'I couldn't accept that idea because the other students would not have time to complete their assignments'. Get the student to imagine how each solution might work if tried.

4. Making the decision, choosing solutions

Hopefully, you will be left with some suggestions or at least one solution that you can both accept. Choose the best. Don't let the student give in to you, acting submissively to get himself off the hook. Work for an effective solution, no matter how small the step may be.

5. Planning how to act on the decision

After a solution has been chosen, a plan must be made to put it into action. Ask, 'What do we both have to do to make this solution work? When will we start? How will we know if the plan is working?'

At this stage a written contract to be signed by teacher and student can be useful. In step 5 you should fix a definite time to review the plan with the student. Making a time shows your intention to follow through and to support the student.

6. Evaluating the success of the solution

It would be unrealistic to suggest that once you have worked through this process with a student your troubles will be over.

Students will sometimes break their commitments, particularly if the problem is a long-standing one. You will be likely to feel let down or that the student is taking advantage of you by making empty promises. It is best, however, to treat the situation as a case of a poor solution rather than a 'bad' student because this position allows you to try again. Don't accept excuses; just move towards a better solution next time. Often plans don't succeed because they require too much change all at once. Aim for small steps towards the final goal.

You may need to work through this process a number of times with a student. In doing so, you are indicating your intention to follow things through. Your commitment can show the student that you have confidence in his or her ability to stick to a plan. You may need to provide the optimism that a student lacks because of previous failure. Being human, you will sometimes feel like giving up on a recalcitrant student. If you do get to desperation point it is often helpful to bring in a colleague who can work through the process with you and the student. The method is not a panacea or a short cut and it won't always work the first time, but it will give you one more positive approach for handling some student-teacher conflicts.

Section Six

Glasser's eight steps of Reality Therapy for the classroom teacher

The American psychiatrist, William Glasser, has developed a systematic way of helping people take control of their lives and solve their own problems — Reality Therapy. From his extensive work in school systems he has shown how Reality Therapy can be used by teachers to help students gain constructive control over their own behaviour. We have briefly described Glasser's eight steps of Reality Therapy below. More detail can be found in Glasser's books and, particularly, in the film *How To Use Reality Therapy in the Classroom* (see References and Resources).

1. Make friends. Ask 'What do you want?' And then ask 'What do you really want?'

Ideally there should be ongoing, positive and courteous relationships with the students where the teacher takes time to share conversation and fun. Talking about enjoyable activities (in other words, having interesting non-problem discussions) is one way to get involved with a student. To help a student 'work it out' the teacher needs some friendship as a basis. The student will need to know from words and actions that the teacher genuinely cares. The teacher can communicate interest and concern by active listening. The teacher's role is to help a student change his own behaviour, not to give the impresion that the teacher can change a student's life. The first step in this process is to get the student to think about what he really wants and how he would like things to be. This means tapping into the picture or ideal the student has in his head. (As in the previous article 'he' is used throughout for the sake of convenience only.)

2. Ask 'What are you doing now?' 'What are you choosing to do now?'

No student will be able to change unless he is aware of his current behaviour and how it contributes to the problem. It is important that the teacher asks the student to describe what he actually does in specific problem situations. This should be done matter-of-factly, and slowly. Sometimes the student will blame others, talk about past events, or discuss his feelings. While it is important to acknowledge the student's feelings and perspective it is essential to bring the focus back onto what the student actually does and the choices he makes about his behaviour. The student can control and change his own current behaviour. It is best to avoid 'why' questions in this process. The student may not know why he does something and may feel obliged to think of a reason and therefore develop the habit of excuse making.

3. Ask 'Is it helping' or 'Is it against the rules?'

Here the teacher asks the student to think about his own behaviour and whether it is good for him and others. It is not the teacher's job to moralise or to judge the student but to help the student evaluate his own behaviour. The goal is to develop a student's ability to make constructive choices. In the end only the student can make the decision to change his own behaviour.

4. Make a plan to get what you want or what you really want.

The teacher's role here is to help the student 'work it out', to develop realistic plans for action once he has evaluated his own behaviour. It is important that the teacher helps the student to make his own plan rather than offering a solution. The teacher may offer suggestions but the student makes the choice. It is best to look for the small realistic steps towards change that have the most likelihood of success. Brainstorming all possible solutions before weighing each one up is a useful way to start.

5. Get a commitment.

After a plan has been made that meets both student and teacher needs it must be carried out. To give the student greater motivation to fulfil his plan, the teacher asks for a commitment. This may be verbal or written. The teacher will only get such a commitment if the student is convinced that the teacher is involved, does care, and will follow up, support, and check how the plan is progressing.

6. Don't accept excuses.

If a problem has been persistent a student may find it hard to keep to his plan and commitment. Ideally the teacher will not give up on the student at this point but rather repeat the process of evaluating the behaviour, getting a new, more workable plan. The important question to ask is not 'why didn't you keep up your plan?' but rather 'are you still going to try (to fulfill your commitment)?'

7. Don't punish but don't interfere with reasonable consequences. Don't criticise.

If the student fails at the first attempt, it is time to help, not moralise. The use of punishment at this point (that is, treatment that causes the student physical or psychological pain) is not appropriate because it breaks the involvement necessary for the student to keep trying. Criticism creates anger and resentment, not change. However, the teacher may allow the student to experience the consequences of irresponsible behaviour, particularly if the student knows and has been involved in making the rules.

8. Never give up. Do not confirm the failure identity.

Sometimes students have failed so often to follow through on their own decisions that they will find it a difficult process. If the failure has been repeated, experience leads the student to expect adults to get frustrated and give up. The teacher needs to convey his or her trust in the student's capacity to change, to convey hope and optimism that the student does have a real chance of success.

Contracting as part of the problem-solving process

Working out differences through discussion may include the development of a contract. A contract can serve to summarise the responsibilities both student and teacher have accepted to alleviate or overcome conflict. Putting a verbal agreement or plan into writing can increase commitment and overcomes the problem of 'What did we decide in that discussion?'

The most useful contracts state clearly and simply what is expected of both parties.

- I, John Green, agree to sit away from Bill and Fred in humanities classes.
- I, Dick Jones, humanities teacher, agree to reduce the number of times I criticise John in front of the class. I will use a private signal when walking close to John's desk if I see a problem in his behaviour.
- We will discuss this plan again on 6 October.

As this example shows, contracts

Section Six

describe specific and realistic behaviours rather than impossible promises like 'I will never talk in class again' or 'I promise I will be good'.

Contracts may also include positive consequences which will follow fulfilment of the agreement and logical consequences or plans for renegotiation if the contract is not successful. It is often desirable for a student's parents to be aware and involved in the preparation of the contract. Ideally the contract will be age-appropriate, clearly worded and provide a positive structure to reduce the likelihood of further conflict.

Section 7:
Planning an approach to confrontations

Although you would expect few confrontations in a school where a positive discipline policy is operating, it is inevitable that some will occur — people being people. To deny this is to bury our heads in the sand. So policy makers need to address the issues of:
- What should be done when confrontations occur?
- How can we prevent the escalation of conflict?
- How can we prevent future confrontations?
- What suggestions will we include in our policy for handling confrontations?

This section provides stimulus material to focus attention on these issues.

Section Seven

'You can't make me': teacher–student confrontations

Verbal or physical confrontations between teachers and students are extremely stressful for all. These emotional showdowns are sometimes avoidable if we are alert to signs in ourselves and our students, but are sometimes inevitable when triggered by events outside the classroom over which we have no control.

We need to know what we can do if a confrontation gets beyond the point of no return, when the student is committed to not giving in at any cost. Being out of control is not fun; students will benefit if they are prevented by a teacher's swift action from harming themselves or others.

Ideally, each school will develop guidelines that provide all teachers not only with the security of knowing possible ways of responding but also with support from colleagues when such situations occur.

There is much to be said for moving away from the view of the teacher on a 'classroom island' to that of the teacher as part of a co-operative team, particularly when emergencies arise. A team of teachers can:

- recognise and work on problems which probably affect more than one teacher;
- pool resources to develop new and creative solutions to the problem or apply old solutions more consistently;
- be supportive of teachers who are attempting new techniques for the first time;
- develop a new perspective on a problem by sharing different points of view;
- foster commitment to following through and reviewing strategies;
- reduce feelings of isolation, helplessness and despair.

The following case studies and vignettes could be used in group discussions to develop strategies for handling emergencies.

A case study

9.30 am: Boy arrives for class. Runs in room, jumps on tables, over other children's work. Teacher takes him quietly to door and asks him to walk in correctly. Child says 'no way' and a few other choice words and runs outside. Teacher returns to class and decides to find the boy once she has settled the class and set them to work. Before long child returns, enters room through window. Class in hysterics. Teacher takes boy by ear, quietly re-explains, 'that's not how we enter a room'. Sits him down and gives him work to do. Teacher turns her back, child races across the room, climbs on cupboard and refuses to get down. Again, class in hysterics. Teacher orders child to get down, 'We sit on chairs not cupboards'. Child again uses choice language.

What would you do now? These questions may give direction to discussion:

- Who should be involved in handling the incident?
- If assistance is to be sought, how might this be done?
- If the student is removed/sent from the classroom, who should be involved? How?
- What might be appropriate consequences?

- Should parents be involved? If so, when?
- How can the relationship between teacher and student be re-established?

Additional case studies

1. Frank and Alan, sitting at the back of the room, have spent most of the time chatting and laughing. When you ask one of them to move to a vacant seat, he refuses.
2. You have quietly asked a student to refrain from talking and he angrily retorts with abusive language questioning your legitimacy and complaining that you always pick on him.
3. You are just about to begin a lesson, and you ask the class to get out their drawing instruments. Nearly half the class haven't brought them, despite the fact that yesterday you especially warned them.
4. You begin a lesson by telling the class that you are about to start a particular new topic. You get moans and groans like 'But we did that last term with Mrs X', or 'Not that again'.
5. Students enter the room and sit down. You're talking away but then it's time for some feedback from the students. You find they have not been listening to you.
6. A student's work is very untidy, disorganised and incomplete. You know he is capable of better work. You ask him to try and improve his work. After a few lessons you don't see any improvement in his bookwork.

Discussion

In discussing the above case studies you may like to use the following format:
1. Select one case study for intensive consideration.
2. Discuss the situation briefly. You may wish to get some group members to act out the problem.
3. What would you do in response to this situation in the short-term? Brainstorm possible responses without evaluation; list them, discuss and evaluate the options.
4. What steps would you take to reduce the likelihood of a similar situation happening again? Brainstorm, then discuss and evaluate.
5. If time permits, you might wish to take the activity a step further, and consider 'What goes on in our thoughts' when we are confronted with crises. Understanding our own reactions to confrontations can help us act more productively. Sometimes we undermine ourselves by negative thoughts or 'self-talk'.
- List unhelpful self-talk (or internal dialogue) you might be in danger of using if you were facing this situation. (For example, 'I can't cope with this. I'm incompetent.')
- Develop some positive self-talk statements you might be able to use as the basis for a constructive response. Record these. (For example, 'It's OK, I can keep cool. I'll think first then react'.)

Prevention is better than cure

In addition to working out guidelines for handling confrontations after they have occurred it's also worthwhile to spend some time considering ways of preventing a minor problem developing into a major incident. When teachers get together there are

Section Seven

many valuable strategies worth sharing.

Robert Pik in Bill Gillham's book *Problem Behaviour in Secondary Schools* (1981), suggests four rules for handling confrontations which could be used as the basis for a group discussion.

1. Decide first whether it is worth risking a confrontation over a particular incident. Has there been a breach of school rules or principles important enough to warrant intervention at that moment or would a quiet word with the student later perhaps be a better course to follow?
2. Leave yourself and the student a gracious way out. There must be room for you both to save face.
3. Remember that threats by a teacher to use physical force or the actual use of physical force will nearly always escalate a conflict very quickly and dramatically and will greatly increase the probability of the student reaching violence.
4. Within a reasonable time after the confrontation, the teacher involved should take the opportunity to talk privately with the student before they are scheduled to come back into contact with one another in the classroom in order to develop a mutually acceptable plan. (The teacher will need to have a problem-solving framework to use in this discussion.)

Pik's guidelines suggest that follow-through after the initial tension has subsided may have a more constructive outcome than forcing the issue at the time.

The exceptions to this are situations of risk or danger where action must be swift. Then it is generally accepted that teachers have a responsibility to intervene.

Section 8:
Aspects of positive policies and practices

Part Two has focused to this point on the processes by which an effective review of discipline policies might be conducted. The following articles and activities are relevant to:
- the selection of content for a positive discipline policy; and
- the implementation of a positive policy.

In this section the articles are designed to help you think about answers to the following questions:
- What areas do we need to include in our discipline policy?
- What does a completed positive policy look like?
- What can we learn from the theory?

Section Eight

Do well disciplined schools have anything in common?

Some schools have relatively few discipline problems and manage the problems which do arise smoothly and effectively. Are these schools just lucky?

The result of an American study of schools with exemplary discipline, described by Wayson et al in their *Handbook for Developing Schools with Good Discipline* (1982), suggests that the answer may lie in the way these schools work. The study identified a number of common characteristics in these 'well disciplined' schools.

1. These schools do many things that have been done by good schools and good educators for a long time; for example, recognise positive behaviour.
2. These schools have fostered good discipline by creating a total environment that is conducive to good discipline rather than adopting isolated practices to deal with discipline problems.
3. Most of the educators view their school as a place where staff and students come to work and to experience the success of doing something well.
4. These schools are student oriented.
5. These schools focus on causes of discipline problems rather than symptoms.
6. Programmes in these schools emphasise positive behaviours and use preventive measures rather than punitive actions to improve discipline.
7. These schools adapt practices to meet their own identified needs and to reflect their own style of operation.
8. The principal plays a key role in making these schools what they are.
9. The programmes in these schools often result, either through happy coincidence or through deliberate design, from the teamwork of a capable principal and some other staff member with personal leadership qualities that complement those of the principal.
10. The staff of these schools believe in their school and in what its students can do; and they expend unusual amounts of energy to make that belief come true.
11. Teachers in these schools handle all or most of the routine discipline problems themselves.
12. The majority of these schools have developed stronger than average ties with parents and community agencies.
13. These schools are open to critical review and evaluation from a wide variety of school and community sources.

These results and others like them give us grounds for optimism. Schools are not the helpless victims of social change. What we do in schools can make a difference!

Eight goals for developing a well disciplined school

This article introduces eight inter-related goals for developing a well disciplined school. The underlying rationale behind all eight goals is that the best discipline can be achieved by a preventive approach — that is, by developing the school curriculum (in the broadest sense of the word) in order to promote desired behaviours.

It would be well worth referring to the *Handbook for Developing Schools with Good Discipline* by Wayson et al, as it discusses the rationale behind the goals and includes many more activities that have been found useful in well disciplined schools. It also gives an inventory that schools could use to identify areas in which they wish to work to improve school discipline and discusses how schools might approach this task. We have quoted, below, the goals from the Handbook and have summarised briefly the rationales and activities it describes.

Section Eight

Goal 1

'To improve the way in which people in the school work together to solve problems'
Rationale:

There will be fewer disruptive behaviours in schools if people have a positive attitude to problem solving.

There can be many problems in a school, but these need not be overwhelming if staff, students and others feel confident that:
- people will work together to solve problems;
- problems can be shared and discussed openly, with criticism being accepted as well intended;
- solutions to problems will be explored and implemented.

Success breeds success. This positive attitude to problem solving will develop as the school successfully tackles and solves its problems.

Example activities:
- Improve staff meetings, making them problem-solving sessions rather than information-giving or 'gripe' sessions.
- Improve informal staff interaction.

Goal 2

'To reduce authority and status differences among all persons in the school'
Rationale:

Authoritarian decision making can lead people to believe that problems of the school are not their responsibility. In contrast, giving people a say in decision making and breaking down any barriers to communication can promote a sense of commitment and responsibility to the school.

Status differences can also provoke negative attitudes that may in turn be the cause for discipline problems.

Example activities:
- Involve staff, students and parents in decision making.
- Have staff/student social events.

Goal 3

'To increase and widen students' sense of belonging in the school'
Rationale:

Students who feel happy in the school, who are involved in school activities, have some responsibility for the smooth functioning of the school and have friends among students and staff are not likely to be discipline problems.

Example activities:
- Increase the number of extra-curricular activities to appeal to more students.
- Give students important jobs in the school. For example, a school beautification plan, or a welcoming team for new students.
- Involve students in decision making, for example, Student Council.
- Assign a staff member to each student to provide a personal contact.

Goal 4

'To develop rules and disciplinary procedures that will promote self-discipline'
Rationale:

Poorly developed rules and poor enforcement procedures can actually cause discipline problems. Discipline procedures should be continually scrutinised to determine whether they are having the desired effects. Punishment, while necessary in some cases, is not a productive way to achieve discipline over the long term and is generally ineffective in developing self-discipline.

People who have to obey or enforce rules should participate in developing them. This will aid understanding of the rules and generate commitment to abide by them. A school also needs clear and fair ways to respond when rule infringements do occur.

Example activities:
- Establish clear, reasonable and enforceable school rules and policies.
- Develop clearly defined programmes for

dealing with discipline, for example, 'time-out' procedures, peer counselling, student advocates.
- Train staff to recognise and acknowledge good behaviour.

Goal 5

'To improve curriculum and instructional practices in order to reach more students'
Rationale:
What is taught and how it is taught will have a powerful effect on people's attitudes and behaviour at school.

Discipline problems will be avoided if:
- curriculum goals are generally accepted by staff, students and parents as worthwhile and attainable;
- instruction begins at the student's level of ability;
- students are not put in a position of repeatedly experiencing failure;
- teaching methods are varied and interesting;
- the curriculum provides choices that recognise staff and student individual styles;
- people care enough to give students constructive feedback;
- students are given help if they cannot do the work.

Example activities:
- Develop a school curriculum that appeals to a wide range of student interests.
- Develop curriculum to meet specific academic deficiencies.
- Create for more students a chance to experience success.
- Train staff to improve curriculum and instruction.

Goal 6

'To deal with personal problems that affect life within the school'
Rationale:
A good school recognises that people will from time to time experience emotions and personal problems that will adversely affect their life in the school. A school can relieve excess pressure by making staff and students feel that they have someone to whom they can tell their problems. Discussion can reveal the cause of discipline and other problems, and if this resides partly within the school, the problem can be corrected or ameliorated. If it seems appropriate, a staff member can help a colleague or friend seek professional help.

Example activities:
- Train staff to deal with conflict, frustration, guilt, anger and other human emotions.
- Set up systems for informal counselling of individuals or groups of students.
- Enlist community agencies to give counselling services to the school.

Goal 7

'To strengthen the interaction between the school and the home'
Rationale:
Teachers who convey their interest in and care about students and their families can help dispel any negative feelings held by parents or students towards the school. This should in turn be reflected in better behaviour and fewer discipline problems in the school.

Understanding of students' lives in the community can help teachers choose an appropriate curriculum; and parents and community groups can greatly enrich a curriculum.

The school has much to gain if the community it serves feels a sense of ownership, pride and responsibility towards the school.

Example activities:
- Invite parents to attend school programmes, fairs, open houses and other events.
- Use the school for meetings — community organisations, adult education and recreation.

- Have students and staff contribute to community events.

Goal 8

'To improve the physical facilities and organisational structure of the school to reinforce the other goals'
Rationale:

Generally, environments that are pleasant for adults and students to work in, and that reflect the interests, culture, and values of students, encourage good behaviour. The more the school environment looks like a workshop, a library, a restaurant, or a conference centre and the less like a prison or an institution, the fewer the problems.

Good organisation of buildings, equipment and of schedules can do much to improve the way people work together, for example, by reducing traffic congestion and providing efficient and pleasant work environments.

Example activities:
- Adjust schedules to permit instruction in large or small groups.
- Cluster units in a large school to make smaller, more personal 'community' groupings.
- Mix grade-level or subject-matter teachers as often as possible to reduce divisions among staff and students.

Critical areas in the development of positive behavioural management strategies

1. Communication and interpersonal relationships
2. Curriculum and teaching methods
3. Rules, behavioural expectations and procedures.

Discipline outcomes are related to procedures in all three strategy areas; not just through rule enforcement. Particular techniques and approaches can be described within each of the strategy areas which are appropriate to the achievement of preventive, reactive and pro-active levels of behavioural management. See the chart over.

Section Eight

Development of a total behaviour management programme

	Communication and relationships	Curriculum and methods	Rules and procedures
Preventive	e.g. What sort of communication do I have with individual students and what sort of class climate exists?	e.g. Do students have an outline of the course/topic and understand its purpose?	e.g. Have I discussed the class rules with the students?
Reactive (Remediation)	e.g. When misbehaviour occurs does my manner and verbal reaction help solve the problem or does it aggravate the situation?	e.g. Do I consider the learning conditions at the time misbehaviour occurs, for the individual/for the group?	e.g. Do I follow agreed-upon procedures?
Pro-active (Long-term developmental)	e.g. Do I teach and develop the skills of discussion and conflict resolution in my classes?	e.g. Are students developing a concept of themselves as successes or as failures in relation to academic achievement?	e.g. Are the rules and procedures reviewed to ensure that they contribute to the school's aims and objectives?

What would a co-ordinated discipline system look like?

Do we know what we are aiming towards in developing an effective discipline policy? The Association of Educational Psychologists in the United Kingdom identified the following features of a co-ordinated student welfare and discipline policy.

1. An organised counselling and pastoral care system.
2. A recognition of training in the use of democratic grievance procedure.
3. Working with parents as true co-operative partners in the education of their children.

4. A recognised support system for staff.
5. Established guidelines for use in cases of dispute.
6. Within-school arrangements for withdrawal or sanctuary from confrontation situations.
7. Report systems used in a constructive way to aid pupils in their achievement of accepted behaviours.
8. The modelling of appropriate behaviour by adult members of the school. Such modelling would include punctuality for school and lessons, manner of speech, respect for alternative viewpoints, facing confrontation without verbal or physical violence, etc.
9. Co-operation with and shared guidelines for action with outside agencies.
10. Incentive systems based on individual effort rather than group comparisons.
11. Curriculum and approaches to discipline agreed to and supported by the staff acting together.

—**Alternatives to Corporal Punishment,** Association of Educational Psychologists (U.K.) 1983.

The above list reflects the importance of developing positive strategies to promote self-esteem and self-discipline as well as developing clear guidelines for managing and resolving problems. A co-ordinated and effective discipline policy will address both.

Chandler High School welfare and discipline policy

The Chandler High School welfare and discipline policy reproduced in part here provides one example of a policy developed through the process described in this book. Over a period of two years the school community worked to develop a welfare and discipline policy that reflected the school's overall aims and objectives. A working party including staff, parents and student representatives co-ordinated policy development activities such as surveys, discussions and in-service programmes.

The document reproduced here is a refinement of earlier versions and was supplemented by resource articles for teachers describing preventive classroom strategies. It was also accompanied by a set of school rules worked out through a process of consultation with students, parents and teachers.

The welfare and discipline policy represented only one dimension of Chandler's efforts to improve the school experience for students and teachers. A concurrent positive change in school organisation involved the introduction of a sub-school system designed to promote better teacher-student relationships and more responsive curriculum development.

Chandler High School does not assume that the task is finished. The policy will require periodic refinement and review. The original set of school rules is being renegotiated in the light of practical experience.

The process of getting people together to plan has been as important as the production of this written document. The school now has a more cohesive and systematic approach to welfare and discipline issues.

Section Eight

Chandler High School Student Welfare and Discipline Policy

Aims and objectives

Chandler High School is committed to the development of the individual as a caring, concerned and contributing member of the community. It recognises that all students are unique individuals, entitled to equal opportunity and continuing support to enable them to realise their fullest possible development — intellectual, personal, physical, creative, social, vocational and moral.

Processes central to achieving the above will include an emphasis upon active student learning tasks, a continuing focus on student success rather than failure and the participation and involvement of parents and the local community.

In addition to the above, it is recognised that student reflection on their own performance, both in terms of themselves and their relationships with others, is vital to the development of self-understanding and tolerance.

Programs will aim at generating immediate enthusiasm for the school, its processes and environment and a continuing enthusiasm for learning beyond school.

C.H.S.'s aims are consistent with William Glasser's philosophy as expressed in "Schools without Failure" (1969) where he states that '. . . every child should have a chance to learn each day' and that a school must strive to be a 'good' place. A 'good' place being one where:
- people are courteous;
- people are involved in relevant work;
- people talk with, not at each other;
- there are reasonable rules and consequences;
- discipline teaches self-responsibility.

The staff at Chandler have recognised that the establishment of a caring relationship with students provides a sound basis for effective communication and problem solving.

Positive, constructive behaviour is encouraged by clearly defined rules, relevant curriculum and caring relationships. The school is committed to creating and maintaining a positive, hospitable environment in which all children can experience a feeling of self-worth and achievement, which matches their needs as emerging adults.

Approaches to student welfare and discipline

School discipline is achieved at two levels:

A. Preventive level — preventive strategies encourage the development of a school climate within which personal responsibility and self-discipline are fostered.

B. Conflict-resolution level — prevention strategies will go a long way in maintaining order but when disruptive behaviour occurs we need the ability to respond positively and effectively.

A. Problem prevention — building a positive and hospitable classroom environment

Classroom teachers have to deal with a wide range of student interest, ability and motivation and need to develop an equally wide range of strategies for dealing both with the curriculm and with problems if they arise. Although tolerance levels vary, minor problems are dealt with in a way that prevents them from becoming major confrontations. Careful preparation, with particular classes in mind, is used as a preventive tool against disruptive behaviour. Reinforcing relationships within the classroom enables teachers to handle problems much more effectively and teachers are urged to constantly evaluate their own methods and results.

B. Conflict resolution

Staff at Chandler have made an effort to avoid the use of many of the traditional discipline techniques which tend to involve negative sanctions. A positive approach to discipline seeks to prevent problems occurring. However, as in any large human institution, problems and conflicts do occur and clear procedures exist as part of school policy in order to resolve them constructively as they arise. They are as follows:

1. Problem-solving interview between student and class teacher:

   The purpose of this interview is to work out a way of overcoming the problem that has occurred and to consolidate a good, working relationship with the student. The student is encouraged to enter into responsible negotiation and to develop self-discipline. These interviews are not always easy because of the emotional involvement of teacher and student or because of lack of training in this area. Some teachers use models for problem solving. Many interviews will be between teacher and student alone, but some may be more effective if a third person is involved as mediator. It is important that teams, co-ordinators, pupil welfare co-ordinators and administrators lend support in this process.

2. Discussion of problem at sub-school level:

   (This may have taken place, in a formal or informal way, before step one was attempted.) If a student has not responded to any of the strategies outlined and the negative behaviour continues, the teacher may decide that the problem can be better handled with consultation and support from others. A meeting of all that student's teachers and the co-ordinator may be arranged to work out constructive plans for dealing with the problem. Parents should be involved at this point and it is helpful if positive contact has already been made.

Section Eight

3. Removal of student from point of conflict:
   If, in spite of the efforts and strategies discussed, the unacceptable behaviour continues, a further step is available. While C.H.S. no longer maintains a permanent supervised 'time-out room' in which a student is removed from all classes, a limited form of time-out is being used by teachers with the co-operation of other team members and in consultation with co-ordinators. This provides both teacher and student with a cooling-off period in which they both have time to reflect on the situation and then work out a mutually acceptable solution.
4. Further problem-solving interview:
   Negotiation at this stage would certainly involve co-ordinators and parents.
5. Involvement of administration:
   At this point if the problem has not been satisfactorily resolved the co-ordinator would approach the Deputy Principal. Further negotiation between all parties would take place.
6. Suspension — eventually leading to an enquiry:
   If the problem persists and the student continues to break the rules of the school, suspension may be considered. Suspension is seen as a time when student, parent and school make time to consider other ways of arriving at a solution. Departmental Regulations determine the way in which suspension may be implemented.
7. Procedures for handling emergency situations:
   The above steps may be by-passed when a situation is considered so serious or dangerous that immediate intervention is required. Assistance should be sought from administration. Certain behaviour may result in immediate suspension.

Section 9:
Rules and consequences

Whenever people are operating in a group, be it family, club, school or work, rules are important to let everyone know:
- how they are expected to behave (raise your hand if you wish to speak);
- what are acceptable limits of behaviour (speed limit 60 kph);
- what is unacceptable behaviour (shop-lifters get court).

When the rules are clearly spelled out, group members benefit from:
- feelings of confidence derived from knowing how to behave;
- feelings of security about how others will behave;
- a reduction in anxiety about how to behave; and
- being able to get on with the task in hand.

In a democratic situation, people have the means to change rules they are unhappy about or to create new rules if the necessity arises.

Problems with school rules have occurred in the past because:
- they were not clearly spelled out (students say they didn't know a rule existed until they broke it);
- there were so many that people couldn't remember them all;
- they were expressed negatively ('Thou shalt not', tells the child what he should not do rather than what he should);
- the reasons were either not obvious or not understood (why shouldn't students smoke if teachers can?)

A three-stage approach

One way of overcoming these problems is to take a three-stage approach:

Stage 1

Identify basic goals for your school. *(See Sections 2 and 4: Values clarification and Meetings and group discussions.)*

You will probably come up with such statements as:
- 'The long-term aim of this school is to develop self-discipline in the students.'
- 'This school should foster caring and co-operation.'
- 'In this school, students should learn respect for themselves and others.'
- 'The school should provide a positive climate for teachers and students.'

Stage 2

Consider what are the rights and responsibilities of each member of the school community in the light of your goals. For example, if you want your school to be a 'positive' place, you might decide that there are three things its members should be able to do. They should be free to experience success, to feel safe, and to learn.

From this, lists need to be constructed which set out the rights and responsibilities for each person in each area. For example:
- if students have the right to learn they also have the responsibility to ensure that others can also;
- if teachers have the responsibility to teach they have the right to expect that they will not be prevented from doing this by the disruptive behaviour of others.

(For an example of this approach, see the pages from Young, Equal in Rights and Responsible, *below.)*

Stage 3

Work out the fewest rules possible in the light of your identified rights and responsibilities.

They might look like this:
- Students will behave at all times in a way which allows others to learn.
- Students will behave at all times in a way which does not endanger their own or others' safety.

Specific rules for your school can then be spelled out if necessary; for example, 'Students will walk their bicycles across the school grounds.' If your few rules are to be known and understood they need to be expressed as simply as possible in a way that indicates the proper behaviour. You may find it necessary to formulate some rules which are prohibitions; for example, 'Smoking is not allowed in classrooms.' The need for this arises when there is debate in the school community over whether or not such an action endangers the safety of others or, indeed, one's own. Consensus or some other form of decision making will need to be used here.

This three-stage approach allows all members of the school community to see that the rules make sense. It should also make it easier for teachers to respond consistently to student behaviour. As it is impossible to have a rule about every situation that might arise, those involved have simply to ask each other the question, 'Is this behaviour consistent with allowing others to learn?'

The more you involve students in formulating the rules, the more likely they will be to understand them and keep them. Ideas for how to involve students may be found in the books listed in Part Three: References and Resources, under the topic heading: Student involvement and responsibility in school and community.

Young, Equal in Rights and Responsible

From Leduc, C. and de Massy, P.R. 'Young, Equal in Rights and Responsible: An interpretation guide to the Quebec Charter of Human Rights and Freedoms prepared for young people in the school setting', Commission des droits de la personne du Quebec, 1981.

Equal in Rights
The Charter says:
  'All human beings are equal in worth and dignity and are entitled to equal protection of the law.' (Preamble)
  And as we shall see . . . the Charter then enumerates the rights and freedoms, and attributes them to 'every person'.
  The Charter says 'Every person has the right to . . .
  Does this statement apply to you?
  Yes, since, according to the Charter, you, too, are a person.
  Every human being is a person, and thus possesses all the rights and freedoms recognised by the Charter.

Equal in Responsibility
The Charter says:
  'Whereas the rights and freedoms of the human person are inseparable from the rights and freedoms of others and from the common well-being.' (Preamble)
  The acknowledgement of the same rights and freedoms to all persons means, as a consequence, that each has the responsibility to exercise their rights in the full respect of the rights of others. Thus, according to the Charter, like adults, you are responsible.
  Like adults, you are obliged to repair the damages that you may cause to others by your failure to respect their rights or freedoms.
  You have rights, the same as those of adults.

Reciprocity

This equality in rights and responsibilities between all the members of a group permits them, taking into account their respective situation, to live a relationship of reciprocity, or in other words, to live a 'relationship in which there is mutual action, influence, giving and taking correspondence . . . between two parties' (The Shorter Oxford Dictionary)

For instance, he or she, young or adult, who exercises the freedom of expression recognised by the Charter, must do it in full respect of the right of others, also recognised by the Charter, to the safeguard of their honour, dignity and reputation.

It is only thus that young people amongst themselves, young people and adults, and adults amongst themselves, can live in the school relationships based on the concept of **Reciprocity.**

The right to the safeguard of one's dignity, honour and reputation

The Charter says:

'Every person has the right to the safeguard of his dignity, honour and reputation.' (Section 4)

This right touches particularly:
- insults, derogatory or derisive remarks
- spreading or contributing to the spreading of negative insinuations, rumors . . .
- police interventions toward young people in the school in a uselessly public way
- content of reports in school records
- making public personal information

Which means that:
- you have the right to be respected, just as adults do. Like adults, you have your dignity, your honour, and your reputation to safeguard.

In a reciprocal relationship,
- the best way to acknowledge this right to others, young or adult, is to accord them as much respect as you expect from them.

Consequences

We all learn from the consequences of our acts. It has generally been believed that if pleasure results we are likely to repeat the act; if pain is the end product, to avoid it. Parents and teachers have acted on this assumption for a long time and have tried to arrange learning experiences so that children are rewarded for approved behaviours.

In the past, schools have tended to focus on listing painful consequences (punishment) for student misdemeanours, hoping that the children would learn quickly not to repeat them. Dreikurs (1972) and Glasser (1969), however, suggest that logical and natural consequences are more effective than punishment in teaching children to take responsibility for their behaviour and to learn from their mistakes.

What are natural and logical consequences and how do they differ from punishment? Natural consequences are those which permit children to learn from the natural order of the physical world; for example, the child who refuses to eat will go hungry. The natural consequence of not eating is hunger.

Logical consequences are those which permit the child to learn from the social order; for example, if a child loses something belonging to someone else he must replace it, or if a child doesn't get up on time and is late for school he is asked to make up time at the end of the day.

Differences between punishment and logical consequences.

Punishment	Logical Consequences
• may not be related to misbehaviour	• related to misbehaviour
• may tell the child he or she is bad	• imply no elements of moral judgement
• focuses on what is past	• concerned with present and future behaviour
• associated with a threat (open or concealed)	• based on logic not retaliation
• demands obedience	• permit choice

Using logical consequences in the school

For logical consequences to be most effective, the child must be able to see the connection between his behaviour and the consequences. A logical consequence should be applied calmly and firmly. If applied aggressively or punitively, consequences can provoke a power struggle between teacher and student or resentment in the student rather than a change of behaviour and attitude. For common classroom or schoolyard problems there should be a clear set of rules worked out in conjunction with the students. The following are examples of logical consequences that could be used by teachers:

Section Nine

If you push or shove in line to get ahead
— you go to the end of the line.
If you fail to put belongings away
— the materials will be put in storage temporarily.
If class assignments are unfinished
— they become part of your homework.
If you do messy work because you are careless
— you must do it again.
If you don't bring your permission slip
— you cannot go on the outing.
If you fight at recess
— you must spend the remainder of your recess sitting quietly alone.
If you vandalise
— you must make restitution; clean up the mess, for example, or pay towards repair.

Before including lists of consequences in your policy, consider if there are any dangers in doing this. You might ask yourself the questions:
- Will there ever be extenuating circumstances for the child's behaviour?
- Can you expect the same consequences to be reasonable for students of widely differing levels of maturity? (Can you attribute the same degree of responsibility to the Year 7 girl who leaves the school grounds without permission and to an H.S.C. student doing the same thing?)

The consequence of having too many and too rigid lists of consequences can be a painful administrative burden for the teacher or principal.

Workshop: Developing consequences

Even if we use preventive strategies and positive consequences there will be occasions on which these are insufficient to bring about the desired changes in behaviour. On these occasions we need to be clear about the consequences we will apply. Preferably, we will seek logical consequences that make sense to the student, where the connection between the misbehaviour and the consequences is an obvious and reasonable one. It is most desirable that students be involved in establishing rules and consequences to increase the likelihood of commitment to and acceptance of them.

Rule (positively stated)	Logical consequences
Students will come to class on time	(a) make up time after school (b) detention (c) loss of free-time privileges (d) parent conference

Workshop task
1. Appoint a recorder
2. Select three behaviours for which you believe consequences should be established (focus on at least two outside the classroom).
3. For each behaviour work out a series of consequences which your group considers to be reasonable reactions to the inappropriate behaviour.

Section Nine

Sample rules from schools

The sets of school rules we have reproduced here are from Yarrunga, Maryborough and South Street, Moe, Primary Schools. **Note that each example is the result of a long collaborative process.** Yarrunga and South Street, Moe, in particular, have paid careful attention to expressing the rules so that young children can understand them and have highlighted student involvement by using the children's illustrations.

Yarrunga Primary School
'Doing the Right Thing at Yarrunga'
To help the school run smoothly we will:
- Be punctual by making sure we come into our classrooms when the bell rings at each recess or lunchtime.
- Always get permission from a teacher to leave the school ground.
- Always order our lunches before school.
- Not go to the shops between 9.00 am and 3.30 pm unless we have a teacher's permission.
- Not bring lollies into the school ground.
- Bring a note from parents if we want to eat cough lollies.
- Only bring plastic drink containers or cans.
- Only wear thongs in an emergency with a note from parents.
- (For the girls) wear sports knicks for phys. ed. sessions but at all other times of wearing them have on a dress, skirt or jeans.

To respect other people and property and ourselves we will:
- Respect each other and our teachers by not fighting, swearing or unnecessarily aggravating them.
- Definitely not spit, punch, kick or bully other people.
- Only throw balls in the school ground because any other objects are dangerous.
- Play cricket, soccer and football only on the oval.
- Use skateboards, billycarts and skates only on the third netball court.
- Stay off the roof, fire hydrants and trees.
- Not play in the front gardens, at the front of the school or anywhere else gardens have been planted.
- Not play games or chase people into or out of the toilets.
- Make it easy for property to be returned by having things clearly labelled with names.
- Respect the property of other people and return anything found to the person who owns it.

South Street, Moe, Primary School
'South Street swings because happiness is remembering the rules'

South Street should be a happy place where children can learn and play without being afraid or worried. If everybody follows these rules no-one will be upset and teachers and parents won't have to growl. The children, teachers and parents at South Street think these are good rules.

Section Nine

SOUTH STREET SWINGS

because

HAPPINESS IS REMEMBERING THE RULES

South Street should be a happy place where children can learn and play without being afraid or worried. If everybody follows these rules no-one will be upset and teachers and parents won't have to growl. The children, teachers and parents at South Street think these are good rules.

South Street children have the right to be able to play safely. Nobody should be frightened by -
- stone throwing.
- fighting, pushing or bullying.
- spitting.
- teasing.
- any other stupid behaviour likely to hurt or annoy others.

If you are unhappy or frightened talk to your friends, your teacher, the teacher on duty, or your parents.

If we all help each other school will be a nicer place.
- be a good sport.
- try to work out problems without arguing.
- be kind to others.
- help new or lonely children.
- don't tease or laugh at others especially when they make mistakes.
- if you see a fight tell the teacher on duty - someone might get hurt.

HAPPINESS IS SOUTH STREET.

Somethings are not suitable or safe at school. You should leave these things at home. -
- glass bottles.
- matches.
- guns, knives and other weapons.
- cricket balls.
- thongs.
- chewing gum.
- computer games and transisters.
- good toys that might get broken or lost.

You will be healthier and happier if you are clean and ready for school. Remember to. -
- brush and comb your hair.
- clean your teeth.
- wash or shower daily.
- change your underwear and socks often.
- wash your hands when you go the toilet.
- eat a good breakfast and lunch.
- make sure you get a good nights sleep.

Children at South Street have the right to be able to learn without being interrupted. - Be a good 'worker'.
- listen to the teacher.
- be polite to your teachers, all visitors and other children.
- keep your books neat and tidy and in their proper places.
- get into line quickly when the bell goes.
- go to the toilet at playtime.

You should be a safe player'. Remember to -
- stay in the playground unless you have permission to leave.
- make sure your bat is only used to hit balls.
- walk your bike to the bike rack.
- play in your own area unless you are a helper.
- play in safe places, unsafe places are in the classroom, in the toilets, up the trees and on the roof.
- keep away from trucks and tractors in the schoolground.
- tell your teacher before you go anywhere with another adult.
- rubbish is dirty and unsafe. Put it in a rubbish bin.
- wear a top that covers your shoulders in summer.

---

132 Positive School Discipline: A practical guide to developing policy

Section Nine

South Street children have the right to be able to play safely.
Nobody should be frightened by:
- stone throwing
- fighting, pushing or bullying
- spitting
- teasing
- any other stupid behaviour likely to hurt or annoy others

If you are unhappy or frightened talk to your friends, your teacher, the teacher on duty, or your parents.

Children at South Street have the right to be able to learn without being interrupted.
- Be a good 'worker'.
- Listen to the teacher.
- Be polite to your teachers, all visitors and other children.
- Keep your books neat and tidy and in their proper places.
- Get into line quickly when the bell goes.
- Go to the toilet at playtime.

You should be a safe player.
Remember to:
- Stay in the playground unless you have permission to leave.
- Make sure your bat is only used to hit balls.
- Walk your bike to the bike rack.
- Play in your own area unless you are a helper.
- Play in safe places. Unsafe places are in the classroom, in the toilets, up the trees and on the roof.
- Keep away from trucks and tractors in the schoolground.
- Tell your teacher before you go anywhere with another adult.
- Rubbish is dirty and unsafe. Put it in a rubbish bin.
- Wear a top that covers your shoulders in summer.

Some things are not suitable or safe at school.
You should leave these things at home:
- glass bottles
- matches
- guns, knives and other weapons
- cricket balls
- thongs
- chewing gum
- computer games and transistors
- good toys that might get broken or lost

You will be healthier and happier if you are clean and ready for school.
Remember to:
- Brush and comb your hair.
- Clean your teeth.
- Wash or shower daily.
- Change your underwear and socks often.
- Wash your hands when you go to the toilet.
- Eat a good breakfast and lunch.
- Make sure you get a good night's sleep.

Section Nine

If we all help each other school will be a nicer place.
- Be a good sport
- Try to work out problems without arguing.
- Be kind to others.
- Help new or lonely children.
- Don't tease or laugh at others, especially when they make mistakes.
- If you see a fight tell the teacher on duty — someone might get hurt.

Happiness is South Street.

Maryborough Primary School

The following are extracts from the policy of Maryborough Primary School, 404. We have included their statement on teachers' rights and responsibilities as being of particular interest.

Conduct code
Introduction
This conduct code is an attempt to stimulate thinking, provide a framework and suggest some strategies for teachers to use when dealing with behavioural difficulties. Hopefully it will allow the teacher to avoid the negative and emotionally charged confrontations which are detrimental to both teacher and child. These strategies will require skill and perseverance but have the potential for creating a positive learning environment, i.e. 'a good place'.

A good place is:
- One where people are courteous, especially the adults. Yelling, sarcasm, and denigration are the exceptions instead of the rule.
- One where communication is practised and not preached. People talk with, not at, each other.
- One that has reasonable rules, rules which everyone agrees on because they are beneficial to the individual and the group, rules which everyone has a democratic stake in because everyone has a say in making and changing the rules as needs arise.
- One where everyone actively supports and participates in an approach to discipline that teaches self-responsibility. An inherent element of this approach is the continuing evaluation of the effectiveness of the conduct code.

Guidelines for staff when rules are broken
Stage one
(a) Discussion
   After self examination the teacher will talk with the pupil to try to reach an understanding.
(b) Removal of privileges
   This will be left to the discretion of the teacher.
   Or
(c) Detention
   This means keeping a child in during recesses, lunch or after school under supervision in accordance with regulations.

Or
(d) Exclusion from grade activities
This means physical isolation within the room or activity centre, or yard.
Note: Parent involvement. Parents may be asked to discuss the problem on an informal basis.

Stage two
Unresolved problems
(a) Parent/teacher/pupil interview
Anecdotal record of discussions and decisions reached to be kept. (Principal to be informed.)
(b) Exclusion from room/yard
In appropriate space with supervision. Sending child somewhere away from the situation (e.g. other classrooms) until child is willing to accept the agreed code of behaviour.
(c) Seeking specialist assistance
For example, Student Services, Special Education Unit, Special Assistance Resource Teacher.

Stage three
Principal, parent/teacher/pupil interview
The teacher will fill out a misconduct form, and will inform parents that a record of interview will be kept on file. Parent and pupil will be informed that unless an acceptable solution is reached then the only recourse for the school is suspension.

Stage four
Suspension (as per Departmental Regulations).

Note:
1. These stages are descriptive rather than prescriptive. The procedure undertaken when a rule is broken will depend on the personnel concerned and the nature of the case.
2. The conduct code itself is intended to be a flexible arrangement where guidelines only are offered to encourage and modify certain types of behaviour.

School rules — Inside/outside
Inside
1. Walk quietly inside.
2. Be respectful of others and their property.
3. When going to another room: Knock, Enter, Wait (KEW)
4. Know which doors you're allowed to enter and exit.
5. We stay outside at lunchtime and playtime and before school.

Outside
1. Respect the games people play, and where they play them.
2. Seek permission to leave the school ground.
3. Play suitable games in suitable areas.
4. Keep the school grounds clean and tidy.
5. Enjoy your recesses and let others enjoy theirs.
6. Consider safety in games.
7. Wheel bikes in the school yard.

Section Nine

8. Climb only on gymnastic equipment.
9. Bring only toys of an acceptably safe nature to school.

Teachers' responsibilities

There are some things you should do without being told. Some of these things you should do for others and some of these you should do for yourself.

1. You have a responsibility to provide a stimulating learning environment. This means providing a meaningful programme to meet the needs of the children.
2. You have a responsibility to make school a good place to be. This means being thoughtful, respectful and courteous to others.
3. You have a responsibility to take care of property.
   This means that you take care of school property and respect your own property and that of others.
4. You have a responsibility to accept school rules. This means observing all safety, playground and classroom rules.
5. You have a responsibility to provide an appropriate social model within the school. This means that our behaviour should reflect the values that we expect of the children.
6. You have a responsibility to see that the conduct code is consistently implemented. This means that all teachers are committed to the smooth running of the school community.
7. You have a responsibility to periodically review the conduct code. This means to constantly access the operation of the conduct code.

Teachers' rights

A 'right' is something which belongs to you and cannot be taken away by anyone. Your colleagues and students have the same rights.

1. You have the right to be an individual at school.
2. You have the right to be respected and treated with kindness at school.
3. You have the right to express yourself.
4. You have the right to a safe school.
5. You have a right to expect your property will be safe.
6. You have a right to expect assistance from any appropriate resource.
   Note: Maryborough Primary School acknowledges indebtedness to the Briar Hill Primary School Policy as a valuable source of ideas.

Section 10:
Discussion papers

Student behaviour: What can psychology tell us?
Liz Freeman

'Nothing is as practical as a good theory'

Complex as human behaviour is we can make some generalisations about how people tick. Researchers have identified patterns of human behaviour that may offer us a greater understanding of student behaviour and the way it can be changed. Ideally during the process of developing a discipline policy a school community will explore psychological theories of behaviour relevant to discipline in schools.

How can you start?

Useful summaries of relevant theories will be found in such books as *Solving Discipline Problems* (Wolfgang and Glickman, 1980) or *Building Classroom Discipline* (Charles, 1981). From these general texts a school can select those theories it might wish to explore in more depth.

Wolfgang and Glickman (1980) suggest that the development of self control in students is a goal that most teachers would endorse. However, teachers may have differing views about how self control can be promoted depending on their beliefs about how children develop and behave. It becomes evident in discussions of discipline that teachers often have different views on how much structure and control children need to develop their potential and behave appropriately. Some teachers view children as naturally developing appropriate behaviour given a supportive environment, others believe that children must be shaped by their environment. Obviously these beliefs will determine how teachers interpret their role in the classroom and may lead them to favour particular management strategies when problems arise. For example if we believe children are largely shaped by their environment we are likely to seek to modify problem behaviour by active alteration of the environment and consequences experienced by the student. We need to become aware of our beliefs and our biases so that we are not limited by them in our interactions with students. Wolfgang and Glickman provide a simple 'Beliefs about Discipline Inventory' to encourage this type of self-evaluation. Although the inventory is not a standardised test, it can be a good discussion starter in meetings on discipline.

Wolfgang and Glickman suggest teachers should investigate psychological approaches to behaviour, recognising that the various approaches depend upon certain assumptions about how behaviour develops and can be changed. They place common psychological theories of behaviour on a useful continuum that ranges from a non-interventionist through an interactionalist to an interventionist position.

Section Ten

Experience shows us that we can't afford to restrict ourselves to one approach with students as the same techniques do not work with all students in all situations. Ideally we will be able to develop a variety of management strategies that will give us more options in working with students. Flexibility and good judgement are the keys to good classroom management.

The following summaries represent a small sample of the useful insights and strategies that can be derived from psychological theories of behaviour. For a fuller appreciation of what various theories have to offer it would be useful to go to the texts listed in Part Three: References and Resources, and to consult the references listed at the end of this article.

A non-interventionist concept

In the non-interventionist category we can find theories which show us how to develop constructive relationships with students.

We are all aware of the societal changes that mean teachers now have to earn their authority rather than being granted it by virtue of their position. Teaching is now a process of building relationships that allow teachers to influence students positively. Thomas Gordon's *Teacher Effectiveness Training* suggests specific skills and strategies which teachers (and parents) can learn to help build and maintain good relationships; for example, active listening, and I-messages.

Not only are good relationships valuable in promoting an effective teaching and learning climate, they also provide a basis for resolving conflicts if they arise.

Interactionalist concepts

Two theories in the interactionalist category which have some valuable concepts for schools are those of Rudolf Dreikurs and William Glasser.

Dreikurs views all behaviour as purposeful. All students' behaviours represent their effort to belong — to gain status and recognition. Student's misbehaviour is seen as a mistaken way to gain recognition. Dreikurs describes four goals of student misbehaviour — attention-getting, power-seeking, revenge and the desire to be left alone. Teachers aware of the Dreikurs framework can use their own gut reactions to work out the goals of student behaviour and decide how to handle the behaviour. Dreikurs's approach suggests that our first reactions to student misbehaviour are not always the best to act upon and he provides alternative strategies. Dreikurs also contrasts the use of logical consequences and punishment to bring about change in behaviour. He favours allowing students to experience the logical consequences of their actions rather than the administering of arbitrary punishments. For Dreikurs, the value of logical consequences is in their educative function.

William Glasser's model, Reality Therapy, highlights humanity's drive to achieve a sense of identity through the satisfaction of the basic human needs for love and recognition. The model explains how students whose basic human needs are not met can develop failure identities and get hooked into such destructive behaviour patterns as acting out or withdrawal. Glasser's book *Schools without Failure* shows how schools can aggravate discipline problems by contributing to failure experiences for students. In his book, Glasser presents an alternative picture of how school programmes can be organised more effectively to meet students' needs for success and to develop responsibility in students. For example, classroom meetings are suggested as one forum in which students can exercise responsibility in evaluating their educational programme, in discussing social issues and in solving everyday problems.

Glasser also offers a counselling framework which can be learned by teachers wishing to help students plan solutions to problems and conflicts — the eight steps of Reality Therapy. The related ten-step discipline programme offers a systematic approach to the management of disruptive behaviour which is based on reality therapy principles. The ten-step discipline programme represents one model of a whole-school discipline system which could be the starting point for schools to develop their own systems.

Interventionist concepts

Behaviour modification is one of the approaches in the interventionist category. Behaviour modification has an optimistic flavour; if behaviour is shaped through the consequences that follow it, new positive behaviours can be developed if we can structure appropriate consequences in the classroom. We can use social-learning principles of reinforcement and modelling to bring about behaviour change. We can learn to 'catch students being good'. Behaviour modification offers the useful idea that if we can strengthen the positive behaviours we want through reinforcement we will simultaneously reduce the opposite negative behaviours. It is often easier and more productive in schools to focus on the development of positive behaviour rather than on the reduction of negative behaviour through the use of controls or sanctions. We need to discover appropriate reinforcers in the school situation to use behaviour modification effectively.

The ideas from the above theories, and many that are not mentioned here, can be incorporated into a school discipline policy. The art of developing a school discipline policy is to orchestrate the various principles of positive behaviour management into a co-ordinated discipline system; to build a bridge between theory and practice.

Section Ten

References:

Charles, C.M., *Building Classroom Discipline: From Models to Practice*, Longman, New York and London, 1981.

Dreikurs, R. and Cassel, P., *Discipline without Tears*, Hawthorn Books, New York, 1972.

Glasser, W. *Schools without Failure*, Harper and Row, New York, 1969.

Gordon, Thomas with Burch, Noel, *T.E.T. Teacher Effectiveness Training*, Peter H. Wyden, New York, 1974.

Wolfgang, G. and Glickman, C., *Solving Discipline Problems: Strategies for Classroom Teachers*, Allyn and Bacon, Boston 1980.

Is discipline a curriculum issue?
Margaret Cowin

'The curriculum is all the arrangements made by a school to promote the development of the child. By "school" we mean the principal and staff acting in consultation with the school council.'
—*The Primary School Curriculum: A Manual for Victorian Schools*, Publications Branch, Education Department of Victoria, 1979.

It is not surprising that under the real day-to-day pressure of dealing with discipline problems schools get caught up in a search for new controls, better sanctions or the elusive magic solution. A reactive putting-out-bushfires position can result, a stance which ignores how the curriculum can prevent discipline problems.

Many writers have argued that some of the practices schools adopt in presenting programmes can contribute to or aggravate student misbehaviour because they leave students feeling unsuccessful and bored. How then can this be avoided?

The definition of curriculum provided above indicates a multiplicity of variables, all of which are recognisable aspects of the normal teaching and learning process. The most obvious of these are:
- what is taught;
- the environment in which it is taught;
- how it is taught;
- how it is organised;
- how evaluation occurs.

A brief look at some of these will indicate their relevance to discipline.

What is taught

The 'what' of school curriculum may include:

facts	(the sun rises in the east)
concepts	('east' describes a particular direction)
understandings	(knowing why things work or why they are important)
skills	(reading, handwriting, investigating)
attitudes	(to enjoy music)
behaviours	(to work co-operatively on a group project)
values	(to respect different religious beliefs)

The content of the curriculum has a positive effect on discipline according to the degree to which the following characteristics are evident:

Students see some sense in the content

Students are generally disposed to put less effort into seeking distractions and more effort into learning if facts and concepts are perceived as being useful, either immediately or in the future. However, note that teachers may need to arouse interest and enthusiasm by clearly explaining such potentiality.

Students are taught directly how to behave

This can happen through a deliberate 'discipline' curriculum; for example, in self-esteem development, social skills training and/or health and human relations courses.

Or it can occur when students are taught the appropriate behaviours for a specific situation and are recognised for using them. The teacher who says 'Chris, I noticed that you worked quietly while I talked to the Principal — that was polite. I appreciated it and so did he!' gives the student two messages — firstly that the behaviour was appropriate, and secondly that it was approved.

Students understand the facts and concepts

Such mastery leads to a sense of being a successful learner. On the other hand, negative consequences — such as feeling and expressing anger — may occur when, for example, students try independent application and cannot manage it because they did not understand an earlier lesson, or when they are faced with the task 'first construct a parallelogram' and they don't know what a parallelogram is. In such a situation the alternatives may be to ask another student (and get into trouble for talking) or find something else — not necessarily productive — to do.

Students see the sense of and enjoy acquiring skills

People who can do something well generally repeat it, as it makes them feel good about themselves. However, skills often take a long time to acquire. Students who compare themselves unfavourably, perhaps with older family members, perhaps with their peers, need encouragement to start and to keep going until they reach the point where mastery brings its own enjoyment. Students who perceive themselves as lacking in skills often make only a token gesture to participate and then become disruptive.

Students don't have teachers' values forced upon them

Some students report that they tune out of school music lessons because their teachers place a higher value on classical than on pop music. Most people react defensively if they feel others are debasing their ideas.

Students feel they can have a say in what is taught

Even very young students can cope with and benefit from making decisions about their own learning (for example, deciding whether to do maths or reading tasks first) with the result that they become more involved and persistent. Some teachers report greater student involvement with a negotiated curriculum as Boomer (1982) has argued.

It can happen, too, that ideas conveyed unintentionally have an unexpected effect on student behaviour. From this hidden curriculum students may learn (and they will react strongly) that it is all right for teachers to eat in classrooms but not for students; that adults do not have to offer reasonable explanations; that mathematics is valued more highly than domestic science (because you never have sports/choir practice in mathematics time). These are not always the things we want them to learn.

Student discipline may also be affected by the ways in which students view those areas of study excluded from the curriculum. If students, particularly older ones, need to have certain information and skills (for example, how to present for a job, or a subject requirement for a higher education course) failure of the school to meet these needs may breed resentment. This resentment may lead to poor social relationships between teacher and pupil, demonstrated perhaps by verbal abuse or, more extremely, by acts of defiance and vandalism.

How the curriculum is organised

Again, positive student behaviour (evidenced by co-operation and success in learning) is likely to result when teachers attend to curriculum sequence and scope.

- When teachers carefully sequence work so that learning progresses in small steps, the task seems manageable and students generally will try.
- When teachers ensure that students have the background knowledge to make new information comprehensible, initial attention at least is likely. It is very easy to 'cut off' when instructors keep using words listeners do not understand. It is also tempting for students to give up when they perceive an enormous gap between what they know and what the rest of the class knows.
- When students are initially given tasks that take into account their existing level of skill, especially for example, in reading, the job seems easier. Working at a higher than comfortable level demands increased energy and therefore is tiring and leads to lack of persistence. As a result the student may become aggressive or withdraw from the situation.
- When students are not confronted at the beginning of the year with what seems an overwhelming amount of work, the goal seems attainable. On the other hand, the bright student may well be marking time while the rest of the class proceeds at a slower rate. A bored intelligent student can be an exceptionally devious mischief-maker.
- When there has been agreement reached among teachers as to what skills, concepts, facts and so on are to be taught in which subject area, unplanned overlap can be avoided. Students lose interest when a unit on 'cities' in social studies is followed by literature related to 'cities' in English followed by a 'city' theme in art, unless these are co-ordinated. Imagine the effect on the unsuspecting art teacher who has done a great deal of preparation for the topic and is greeted, when introducing the theme, with howls of dismay from the class.
- When there has been co-ordination about the amount of homework expected of students and the day it is due to be handed in, students are more likely to feel that the demands on their time are reasonable. Students have rights too and they are becoming increasingly aware of them. Almost intolerable demands on leisure time are made by some schools with the result that incentive to continue learning is killed.

How the curriculum is taught

Rarely do two teachers translate the same curriculum proposal into equally valuable learning experiences for their students. Those who get greater involvement, pleasure and success for themselves as well as for students, pay attention to such factors as:
- varying the methods of presentation — sometimes using direct teaching, at other times using reference books or films, sometimes games — thereby avoiding the overuse of assignments and worksheets; boredom leads to idleness and trouble;
- knowing the developmental levels of the students along many different lines; for example, with young students, recognising that their attention span is limited and so planning to change activities frequently; with older students, taking into account their need for increasing opportunities for independence;
- not dominating the classroom by talking at the students but allowing them time to talk with each other and with the teacher;
- being well prepared and enthusiastic;
- having the students actually involved, not just sitting passively 'listening' (after all, how do you know they are?);

- having clear objectives for lessons;
- within the classroom, organising smooth transitions from one activity to another;
- making expectations about tasks clear;
- indicating respect for each student by getting to know their names and interests as soon as possible; continually demonstrating this respect by the manner in which students are spoken to;
- involving students in suggesting how they should learn particular topics; Glasser (1965) and Dreikurs (1972) suggest holding classroom meetings not only to prepare the ground for new topics but also to work out how they will be learned and evaluated;
- not going so quickly that the student can't keep up;
- using humour. Glasser is one of many educationists who plead for teachers and students to have fun together. (It is hard to be angry with someone when you share a joke.)

Maslow (1972) suggests that we have common needs which we all strive to meet; for example, needs for safety and security, to belong, to feel adequate, to have confidence, for attention, for knowledge. In one way or another each of the strategies suggested above, when used positively, can enable learners to meet those needs; students will feel safe and secure, for example, if class lessons go in an orderly fashion with known, set procedures for dealing with routines (distributing materials, tidying up) clearly identified and established. Conversely, where the school situation does not provide such opportunities, students will create their own. The 'clown of the class' can be identified as seeking attention, the 'clinging vine' as desperately wanting to belong, the 'restless fly-catcher' as needing to establish secure limits for behaviour.

Teachers have needs too, many of which may only be met if students behave appropriately. Some modifications in the way in which the curriculum is taught, taking into consideration the desirability of meeting student needs, could improve teachers' chances of meeting their own needs as well.

The environment of teaching

The 'environment of teaching' refers both to the human as well as to the physical context in which learning takes place.

Teachers can present opportunities for learning experiences in a variety of different contexts — all of which have the capacity to contribute to the degree to which students behave co-operatively.

- Teachers themselves contribute to the human environment of the school. By their actions they convey to students whether or not they are interested, caring, consistent, humane. Students are far less likely to set out deliberately to disrupt the class of someone they like (adolescents tend to have very strong likes and dislikes).
- Teachers contribute to making the school environment a safe and secure one for students by working with them and their parents to provide an agreed upon set of rules. Where students think these are reasonable and administered consistently they will even agree that punishment is 'fair enough'. Rebellion emerges when young people feel adults can pluck a rule out of the air to meet a particular situation.
- Teachers can organise the class so that at different times they use both individual

and group teaching methods. The groups may be of many different kinds — informal groups, interest groups, those based on level of skill, or whole classes. Where pupils know how to behave in such groups, learning may be facilitated. Where the needs of the student are not met by this arrangement (for example, if the work set for the group is too difficult) disruption is likely to occur.
- The way in which the classroom is physically organised for teaching can similarly create or prevent problems. Furniture that is too large or too small leads to discomfort and restlessness; narrow passageways contribute to tripping and pushing; inadequate lighting or over-heating can cause tiredness and irritability. Materials locked away may convey messages of distrust; damaged or vandalised desks and equipment say, 'Others too have felt your disenchantment'. Some local schools have reported positive effects when students have been allowed to become involved in organising and decorating their classrooms.
- Playground organisation (an arrangement intended to promote physical development) is similarly important. There are generally fewer fights when there is room to move and activities are available. As it's almost impossible to increase the size of the playground, strategies such as staggered recess times can be used to overcome a problem.
- By making use of camps and excursions, environments other than the school can be used creatively to capture student interest and involvement.

How evaluation occurs

For students the unkindest cut of all must be to be tested on material that the teacher did not teach. The consequent feelings of powerlessness and of being hardly done by rarely lead to an increased commitment to learn.

When teachers are concerned to prevent this and to ensure that evaluation is constructive:
- They assess constantly. During and at the end of each lesson they ask themselves, 'Is the student interested in this task? What is he doing to convince me that he is learning?' When a student is obviously uninterested or failing to make progress these teachers do not persist with the same strategies.
- They give the students immediate feedback about their work and provide the opportunity to make any necessary improvements without penalty. What's wrong with an eraser after all?
- They respect the students' dignity when correcting them. These teachers operate by the rule of dealing with strengths in public and weaknesses in private.
- They let the student know on what basis any formal assessment is going to be made. Some schools are encouraging the participation by students in descriptive self-evaluation.
- They select formal assessment measures that actually reflect the curriculum taught, not tests written by someone else. (If external exams are to be taken, responsible teachers ensure that they teach the appropriate syllabus.)
- They don't penalise a student (for example, a hesitant reader) by requiring a great deal of reading in the assessment process. They may, perhaps, give the student an opportunity to do the test orally. Failure to do this not only penalises the child who may have learned, it also reflects badly on the teacher who taught well but assessed poorly.

Section Ten

- They ask themselves, 'Are closed-book examinations the best or only measure of knowledge?'

Teachers have a multiplicity of variables at their disposal which can be adapted to achieve effective teaching and learning. This article has put the proposition that the same variables that contribute to effective teaching can also contribute positively and preventively to student discipline.

In short, the argument is that discipline is a curriculum issue.

References:

Boomer, Garth, *Negotiating the Curriculum: A teacher-student partnership*, Ashton Scholastic, Sydney, 1982.

Dreikurs, R. and Cassell, P., *Discipline without Tears*, Hawthorn Books, New York, 1972.

Glasser, W., *Schools without Failure*, Harper and Row, New York, 1965.

Maslow, A.M., 'A theory of human motivation', in *Human Dynamics in Psychology and Education*, Hamachek D.E. (Ed.), Allyn and Bacon, Boston, 1972.

Corporal punishment
Margaret Cowin

Corporal punishment is not an option as a discipline strategy in Victorian Government schools. However, people hold strong opinions about its value and it is highly probable that members of your school community may even be in favour of corporal punishment. Talking about conflicting beliefs and bringing them out into the open can provide a useful beginning to the process of developing a discipline policy. The summary of points below could provide useful pre-reading for such a discussion — a discussion which aims to recognise that people have a right to their own views but are required to reach agreement on a school discipline policy that does not include corporal punishment.

Reasons advanced for using corporal punishment:
1. It works; in other words, it stops the offending action.
2. It is a deterrent; in other words, when a child associates the unpleasantness of corporal punishment with a particular deed he will be unlikely to repeat it.
3. It helps the child develop self-control.
4. It demonstrates to the child that the adult is in control.
5. It sets an example to others.
6. It teaches young children to understand, because one cannot reason with them.
7. 'It's the only punishment these kids understand!'
8. It fulfills the adult's moral responsibility towards the child. For some, this has a Biblical basis.
9. It exacts retribution.
10. It develops conscience.
11. It 'makes a man of a boy'.
12. Schools will become chaotic without corporal punishment.

Reasons advanced for contrary position:
1. It does not completely eliminate the undesired behaviours; it merely slows down the rate at which they occur.
2. It teaches the child 'how not to get caught' rather than the appropriate behaviour.
3. It creates additional stress in the student and this may interfere with learning (although it may relieve tension in the punisher).
4. It can increase anxiety and withdrawn behaviour in the observers of the act.
5. It imposes external control rather than allowing the gradual development of internal control. Hence, self-control will be delayed in its development.
6. It conveys a message that 'might is right'.
7. It does not offer a rationale for desisting from certain behaviour, nor does it offer acceptable behaviours as alternatives.
8. It creates frustration or aggression in the child because of inability to retaliate, particularly if the student believes the punishment was unjust.
9. It arouses aggression which may find its outlet in a variety of ways — resentment, vandalism, non-compliance.

Section Ten

10. It can arouse anxiety about school in general, if the reason for the punishment is not known by the student.
11. It may, paradoxically, become pleasurable — through attention gained or sexual associations with the act.
12. It provides information for the student as to what 'stirs' the teacher.
13. It is unacceptable to some religious groups.
14. It interferes with children's rights; for example, the right of children to freedom from fear of psychological and physical harm or abuse, particularly at school which they are compelled to attend.
15. It is not necessary as there are plenty of alternative punishments which have less danger of unwanted side effects.
16. It is discriminatory in that girls have never been allowed to be strapped.
17. It is a violent act. Schools should lead the way in promoting less aggression in society as a whole.
18. It is only a small aspect in a total discipline system. Discipline and self-discipline can be achieved without it.

Self-esteem: What is it? How can we enhance it?
Ailsa Drent

If we are asked to describe ourselves, many attributes come to mind — who we are, where we live, what we believe, what we like and dislike, what talents we may have to offer, and so on. The perception that we ourselves have of these attributes can be defined as our self-concept. Alternatively, self-concept has been described as the concept of oneself as a performer, and related to our sense of self-respect, confidence, identity and purpose. Self-esteem, a term often used interchangeably with self-concept, relates to the value we hold of ourselves, independent of performance and measured attributes.

The self-concept is learned rather than inherited, and is developed sequentially from infancy. Psychologists stress the need for favourable development as it is integral to all other aspects of human learning and development. Recent findings suggest that not only is a sequential process involved, but that it commences as an image the young child forms as he or she observes the reactions of important others. Further, when feedback from one of these individuals is lacking, the child may feel insecure in some situations. Hence, clarification of these doubts and insecurities will need to take place.

Reasoner (1982) has identified five major components of self-esteem and believes that they match criteria for success in adults. They are, as follows: a sense of security, a sense of identity, a sense of belonging, a sense of purpose, and a sense of personal competence.

Each component has specific input requirements so that maximum outcomes can be gained. Parents and teachers, as adults, have crucial roles to play. Philosophically, two underlying principles are identified. Firstly, that children be related to as important and responsible individuals; and secondly, that children have rights and deserve respect as individuals.

In action terms, many strategies are available to us. In order to develop secure children, we need to develop a trusting relationship. Limits and rules need to be negotiated, delineated and consistently adhered to. To develop identity, we must recognise strengths, provide feedback and constantly communicate with caring and love. To nurture a sense of belonging, we need to create caring environments at home, school and in the community. Such environments will foster feelings of being accepted, nurtured and wanted. For the development of a sense of purpose realistic expectations and goals need to be set and negotiated, thus planning for success and the accompanying increase in confidence.

Finally, the important area of personal competence; we need to teach decision-making skills and self-evaluation, and also to provide rewards and recognition. Many exciting, creative strategies and programmes exist to assist us further. Recent findings suggest that one such example, cross-age tutoring, not only increases academic competencies, but also enhances self-concept, self-discipline and motivation. Linked to that notion is the use of adults as mentors, key-workers and skill-sharers. Other programmes considered invaluable include classroom meetings, problem-solving approaches to curriculum and relationship issues, social skills training, values clarification procedures, and student participation programmes.

Section Ten

All of these processes rest on the two guiding principles identified earlier, and all have been shown to effectively contribute to at least one of the five components of self-esteem.

Reference:

Reasoner, R.W., *Building Self-esteem*, Consulting Psychologists Press, California, 1982.

Section Ten

Social skills: Can we teach students to behave?
Liz Freeman

A school that is committed to a preventive approach to discipline will want to find ways of promoting 'pro-social' behaviours among students. We could speculate that it is particularly necessary for schools to do this because social changes have weakened the influence of the other traditional socialising institutions, the family and the church.

In practice, many schools teach the value of behaviours by default through the example of teachers' own conduct in the school. This hidden curriculum can work positively where teachers practice what they preach. But sometimes this informal teaching goes astray. For example, a teacher may argue the importance of students' being on time for class while she herself arrives late. From our experience, and according to research on modelling, actions are likely to have more impact than words; so that actually the lesson learned here may be that punctuality is not particularly important.

This example highlights the need to teach social behaviour in a conscious, planned and systematic way, so that we have more chance of teaching what we want to teach. Many schools have acknowledged the influence of teacher behaviour on student behaviour by developing codes of responsibilities for teachers as well as students. Many schools have also recognised the need to allow curriculum time for learning about effective relationships through pastoral care and human relations programmes. An area which has been less explored by schools is the direct teaching of specific social skills, or social skills training.

What is social skills training?

Social skills training is based on the assumption that social behaviour involves learned skills which can be identified and taught systematically.

It stresses the development of interpersonal skills that do not infringe on the rights of others. A typical definition of social skills is:
'The ability to interact with others in a given social context in specific ways that are socially acceptable or valued and at the same time personally beneficial, mutually beneficial or beneficial primarily to others'. (Combs and Slaby, 1977).

Social skills training includes programmes designed to teach students how to:
- make friends;
- deal with criticism, teasing and bullying;
- be assertive without being aggressive;
- plan and organise themselves;
- solve problems;
- identify alternative courses of action;
- understand cause and effect in social behaviour.

In social skills programmes, complex behaviours like these are taught and developed on the basis of observation and training in basic verbal and non-verbal behaviours such as initiating conversation, asking questions, eye contact, posture, and the volume, rate and intensity of speech.

Social skills training involves very direct teaching based on the following steps:

Section Ten

- definition in specific behavioural terms of the behaviour to be taught;
- assessment of the existing level of competence;
- teaching of the behaviours that are lacking;
- evaluation of the results of teaching;
- provision of opportunities for practice of behaviours in new situations.

Actual teaching sessions include instruction, modelling or demonstration, rehearsal by students, and feedback and practice. Because sessions require active participation of students, ideally the teaching takes place in small groups to allow for the participation of all students in rehearsing behaviours.

While social skills training has a place in the teaching of all students — at the developmental and preventive level — it also has a useful place in assisting students experiencing social difficulties.

Aggressive, angry, isolated and immature students all have one thing in common. Besides being a headache for adults, they all lack the social skills that would enable them to achieve personal satisfaction through constructive relationships with others. Social skills groups can be developed with the assistance of consultants to help these students.

Social skills training is a relatively new and promising field. A number of useful references may be found in Part Three: References and Resources.

Part Three:

References and Resources

References

Andrews, Greg, Bryant, Ralph and Pankhurst, John, *School Policy Manual: Practical Techniques for Involving the Community in Policy Development*, School Community Interaction Trust, Victoria, 1981. (Available from 2 Blanche Court, East Doncaster 3109.)

Blachford, Kevin, *Destination: Decisions*, Curriculum Branch, Education Department of Victoria, 1984.

Boomer, Garth, *Negotiating the Curriculum: A teacher–student partnership*, Ashton Scholastic, Sydney, 1982.

Canfield, J. and Wells, H., *100 Ways to Enhance Self-concept in the Classroom*, Prentice-Hall, New Jersey, 1976.

Charles, C.M., *Building Classroom Discipline: From Models to Practice*, Longman, New York and London, 1981.

Chase, Larry, *The Other Side of the Report Card*, Goodyear, California, 1975.

Cohen, David and Harrison, Marelle, *Curriculum Action Project: A Report of Curriculum Decision-making in Australian Secondary Schools*, Curriculum Action Project, School of Education, Macquarie University, North Ryde, New South Wales, Australia, 2113.

Combs, M.L. and Slaby, D.A., 'Social skills training with children, in Lahey, B.B. and Kazdin, A.E. (Eds.), *Advances in Clinical Child Psychology*, Vol 1, Plenum Press, New York, 1977.

Dreikurs, R. and Cassel, P., *Discipline Without Tears*, Hawthorn Books, New York, 1972.

Education Department of New South Wales, *Self-discipline and Pastoral Care*, (Thomas Report), New South Wales, 1981.

Education Department of Victoria, *The Primary School Curriculum: A Manual for Victorian Schools*, Education Department of Victoria, 1979.

Education Department of Western Australia, *Discipline in secondary schools in Western Australia*. Report of the committee of enquiry into discipline in secondary schools in Western Australia under the chairmanship of Mr H. Dettman, Education Department of Western Australia, 1972.

Fox, R.S. and others, *School Climate Improvement: A Challenge to the School Administrator*, Phi Delta Kappa, Indiana, undated.

Gillham, B. (Ed.), *Problem Behaviour in the Secondary School*, Croom Helm, London, 1981.

Glasser, W., *Schools without Failure*, Harper and Row, New York, 1969.

Gordon, Thomas with Burch, Noel, *T.E.T.: Teacher Effectiveness Training*, Peter H. Wyden, New York, 1974.

Hall, G.E., 'The Concerns-based Approach to Facilitating Change', in *Educational Horizons*, 1979.

References

Hall, G.E., Wallace, P.C. Jr. and Dossett, W.A., *A developmental conceptualization of the adoption process within educational institutions*, University of Texas, Research and Development Center for Teacher Education, 1973. Eric No. ED 095 126.

Joyce, B. and Showers, B., 'Improving In-service Training: The Messages of Research', in *Educational Leadership*, 1980.

Lawrence, J., Steed, D. and Young, P., 'Coping with disruptive behaviour', in *Special Education: Forward Trends*, Vol 10, No 1.

Leduc, C. and de Massy, P.R., *Young, Equal in Rights and Responsible*, Commission des droits de la personne du Quebec, 1981.

Maslow, A.H., 'A theory of human motivation', in *Human Dynamics in Psychology and Education*, Hamachek, D. (Ed.), Allyn and Bacon, Boston, 1972.

Pfeiffer, J.W. and Jones, J.E., *A Handbook of Structured Experiences for Human Relations Training*, University Associates Press, Iowa City, 1969, Vols 1-5.

Reasoner, R.W., *Building Self-esteem*, Consulting Psychologists Press, California, 1982.

Wayson, W.W., Devoss, G.G., Kaeser, S.C., Lasley, T. and Pinnell, G.S., *Handbook for Developing Schools with Good Discipline*, Phi Delta Kappa, Indiana, 1982.

Williams, Trevor and Batten, Margaret, *The Quality of School Life*, Australian Council for Educational Research, Victoria, Australia, 1983.

Wolfgang, G. and Glickman, C., *Solving Discipline Problems: Strategies for Classroom Teachers*, Allyn and Bacon, Boston, 1980.

Resources

This section is organised under topic headings. Under each area you will find lists of available:
- Books and reports
- Booklets
- Short articles
- Periodicals
- Kits
- Films and videos

Topic headings

Reports and general issues relating to discipline
Leadership and the process of change in schools
Evaluation
Group participation in decision making
Parent and community participation
Student involvement and responsibility in school and community
Staff development and in-service training
Curriculum and teaching methods as preventive approaches to discipline
School climate and organisation
Student welfare
Interpersonal skills (for teachers)
Assertion training (for teachers)
Self esteem, social skills training and values clarification (for students)
School rules

Behaviour management:
- Resources covering a range of models
- Assertive models
- Behaviour modification
- Cognitive behaviour modification and Rational Emotive Therapy
- Glasser's Reality Therapy approach
- Dreikurs and Systematic Training for Effective Teaching
- Thomas Gordon and Effectiveness Training
- Transactional Analysis

Resources

Reports and general issues relating to discipline

Books and reports
Doyle, J.J., Stringer, P.H. and Lucas, D., *Alternatives to Corporal Punishment*, Association of Educational Psychologists, 3 Sunderland Road, Durham, U.K. DH12 LH, 1983.

Education Department of New South Wales, *Pupil Behaviour and Discipline: Support Materials*, NSW Department of Education, 1982.

Education Department of New South Wales, *Self Discipline and Pastoral Care*, Report of the Committee of Enquiry into Pupil Behaviour and Discipline (Thomas Report), Government Printer, NSW, 1981.

Education Department of Victoria, *Report of the Working Party on Abolition of Corporal Punishment*, Materials Production, Curriculum Branch, Education Department of Victoria, 1983.

Education Department of Western Australia, *Discipline in secondary schools in Western Australia* (Dettman Report), Report of the committee of enquiry into discipline in secondary schools in Western Australia under the chairmanship of Mr H. Dettman, Education Department of Western Australia, 1972.

Gillham, B. (Ed.) *Problem Solving in the Secondary School*, Croom Helm, London, 1981.

Newell, Peter, *A last resort? Punishment in Schools*, Penguin, Hammondsworth, 1972.

Ritchie, Jane and Ritchie, James, *Spare the Rod*, George Allen and Unwin, Sydney, 1981.

Wayson, W.W., Devoss, G.G., Kaeser, S.C., Lasley, T. and Pinnell, G.S., *Handbook for Developing Schools with Good Discipline*, Phi Delta Kappa, Indiana, 1982.

Short articles
Duke, Daniel L. 'Adults Can be Discipline Problems Too!' in *Psychology in the Schools*, 15 (4), 1978.
In a suburban high school study, it emerged that concerns of teachers and administrators centred more on adult than on student behaviour. Six categories of adult discipline problems were identified: inconsistent rule enforcement, noncompliance with discipline policies, insensitivity to students, lack of discipline data, lack of classroom management skills, and inadequate administration of disciplinary policies.

Lasley, T.J. and Wayson, W.W., 'Characteristics of Schools with Good Discipline,' in *Educational Leadership*, 40 (3), 1982.
A discussion of some of the results of the Phi Delta Kappa Commission on Discipline. For further information about this study, see the Part Two, Section 8 articles 'Do well disciplined schools have anything in common' and 'Eight goals for developing a well disciplined school'.

Lewis, Ramon and Lovegrove, Malcolm, 'Pupils on Punishment' in *SET: Research Information for Teachers*, No. 1, 1983, Item 10, NZCER and ACER.
> Discusses results of a study of students' perceptions of teachers' classroom management procedures.

Moore, Timothy, 'Drawing the Line: Child Development and its Relevance for Discipline', in *Inter View*, No. 12, 1984, Education Department of Victoria.
> All children need clear limits which are benignly enforced. The limits set should be age appropriate and children need to be given true independence within these limits. The author argues that these principles apply to children of all ages, but goes on to discuss differences in the ways they need to be applied to meet the discipline needs of children of different ages.

Survey Report, 'Discipline in New Zealand state secondary schools', in Education (NZ), 29 (3), 1980.
> This report summarises survey information about discipline in New Zealand secondary schools.

Periodicals

Discipline, The National Center for the Study of Corporal Punishment and Alternatives in Schools, 833 Ritter Hall South, Philadelphia, Pennsylvania, 19122, USA.

Films and videos

Corporal Punishment — Kids Ask Why, NSW, 20 minutes.
> Video in which NSW school children interview a number of people regarding their views on corporal punishment and also discuss their relationships with teachers and the importance of good communication.

I'd Like a Word with You, Britain, 1979, 28 minutes.
> John Cleese illustrates some ways in which a discipline interview can be mishandled and the more appropriate approaches. Filmed in business settings. Fun.

Spare the Child, Australia, 1980, 12 minutes.
> Film looking at some issues relating to parental discipline. Teenagers are mentioned briefly but most examples are with young children.

Leadership and the process of change in schools

Books

Archibald, Jack, *We Did This Ourselves: On Leadership in Schools*, Ashton Scholastic, Sydney, 1975.

Broadbent, R.F. (Ed.) *Education Policy Making in Australia: Selected papers from the Australian College of Education Conference 1982*, The Australian College of Education, Carlton, Victoria, 1982.

Fox, R.S. and others, *School Climate Improvement: A Challenge to the School Administrator*, Phi Delta Kappa, Indiana, undated.

Resources

Fullan, Michael, *The Meaning of Educational Change*, Teachers College Press, Columbia University, 1982.
Havelock, Ronald G., *The Change Agent's Guide to Innovation in Education*, Educational Technology Publications, New Jersey, 1973.
Hersey, P. and Blanchard, K.H., *Management of Organisational Behaviour: Utilising Human Resources*, Prentice-Hall, New York, 1982.
Hoy, W.K. and Miskel, C.G., *Educational Administration Theory Research and Practice*, 2nd edition, Random House, New York, 1982.
Owens, R.G., *Organisational Behaviour in Schools*, Prentice-Hall, Englewood Cliffs, 1970.
Sergiovanni, T.J. and Starratt, R.J., *Supervision, Human Perspectives*, McGraw-Hill, New York, 1982.
Schmuck, R. and Runkel, A, *The Second Handbook of Organizational Development in Schools*, Mayfield, 1977.
Waller, W., *The Sociology of Teaching*, John Wiley and Sons, Sydney, 1976.
Wayson, W.W., Devoss, G.G., Kaeser, S.C., Lasley, T. and Pinnell, G.S., *Handbook for Developing Schools with Good Discipline*, Phi Delta Kappa, Indiana, 1982.

Short articles

Cowin, M., *Planning innovation within a school: some considerations*, Education Department of Victoria, Student Services.
Hall, G.E., 'The Concerns-based Approach to Facilitating Change', in *Educational Horizons*, 1979, 57.
Hall, G.E., Wallace, P.C. Jr. and Dossett, W.A., 'A developmental conceptualisation of the adoption process within educational institutions', University of Texas, Research and Development Center for Teacher Education, 1973 Eric No. ED 095 126.
McDaniel, Thomas, 'Well Begun Is Half Done, A school-wide project for better discipline', in *SET: Research Information for Teachers*, No. 1, 1983, Item 9. In several in-service days prior to the school year, a school staff learns about and practises discipline techniques. The article includes a useful chart about the properties of good and bad school rules.

Films

Decisions, Decisions, Britain, 1978, 28 minutes.
John Cleese illustrates some of the problems that arise when there is inadequate consultation and fact gathering prior to making decisions.
Meetings, Bloody Meetings, Britain, 1976, 34 minutes.
A John Cleese film illustrating the need for effective planning and preparation prior to a meeting and for strategies to keep discussions productive and more satisfying for participants.

Resources

Evaluation
Books
Atkinson, J.M. and Beeson, G.W. (Eds.), *Policies and Practices for School Evaluation in the Eighties*, Rusden Centre for Studies in the Curriculum, Clayton, Victoria, 1981.
Blachford, Kevin, *Destination: Decisions*, Curriculum Branch, Education Department of Victoria, 1984.
Brennan, Marie and Hoadley, Ruth, *School Self Evaluation*, School Improvement Plan Secretariat, Education Department of Victoria, 1984.
Education Department of Victoria, *The Primary School Curriculum: A manual for Victorian Schools*, Publications Branch, Education Department of Victoria 1979.
Education Department of Victoria, *School Review Resource Book*, Secondary Schools Division, Education Department of Victoria, 1980.
Fraser, Barry J. and Edwards, John F., *Guide to Evaluation of School-based Projects*, Northern Districts Education Centre, Cheltenham, NSW, 1982.
Groundwater-Smith, Susan and Nicoll, Vivienne, *Evaluation in the Primary School*, Novak, Sydney, 1980.
Hughes, P. and others, *A Guide to Evaluation*, Curriculum Development Centre, Canberra, 1980.
Shipman, Marten, *In-school Evaluation*, Heinemann, London, 1979.

Annotated bibliographies
Education Department Library, *Select Reading List No. 1: School-based Evaluation*, Education Department Library, Education Department of Victoria, 1983.
McConachy, Diana, *The Teachers as Evaluators Project, Bibliography, Parts I and II*, Curriculum Development Centre, Canberra, 1978 and 1979.

Group participation in decision making
Books
Delbecq, A.L., Van de Ven, A.H. and Gustafson, D.H., *Group Techniques for Program Planning: A guide to nominal group and delphi processes*, Scott, Foresman and Company, USA, 1975.
Blachford, Kevin, *Destination: Decisions*, Curriculum Branch, Education Department of Victoria, 1984.
Pfeiffer, J.W. and Jones, *The 1973 Annual Handbook for Group Facilitators*, University Associates, San Diego, 1973.

Short articles
Arends, Richard I., The Use of Task-force Planning for School-based Improvement Efforts, *Planning and Changing*, 13, (4), 1982.

Resources

Film
Decisions, Decisions, Britain, 1978, 28 minutes.
Meetings, Bloody Meetings, Britain, 1976, 34 minutes.
>For abstracts of these two films see the topic heading: Leadership and the process of change in schools.

Group Think, McGraw-Hill Films, USA, 1973.
>Group decision making can become ineffective when the group is excessively close knit or cohesive and unable to tolerate divergent opinion or information.

Parent and community participation

Books
Andrews, Greg, *The Parent Action Manual*, School Community Interaction Trust, 2 Blanche Court, Doncaster, Victoria, Australia.

Losen, Stuart M. and Diament, Bert, *Parent Conferences in the Schools: Procedures for Developing an Effective Partnership*, Allyn and Bacon, Boston, 1978.

Pettit, David, *Opening up Schools: School and Community in Australia*, Penguin Books, Australia, 1980.

Research studies (books)
Cyster, R., Clift, P.S. and Battle, S., *Parental Involvement in Primary Schools*, National Foundation for Educational Research in England and Wales, 1979.

King, Ray and Watson, Ken (Eds.), *Parental Involvement in Australian Schools: A follow-up study*, The Hills Education Study Group, Sydney, 1976.

Lynch, James and Pimlott, J., *Parents and Teachers*, School Council Research Studies, Macmillan Education, London, 1976.

Booklets and longer articles
Andrews, Greg, Bryant, Ralph and Pankhurst, John, *School Policy Manual: Practical Techniques for Involving the Community in Policy Development*, School Community Interaction Trust, 2 Blanche Court, Doncaster, Victoria, Australia, 1981.

Beare, Hedley, *Lay Participation in Education*, Paper delivered to the Australian Council of State School Organisations Conference at Surfers Paradise, Queensland in October 1974.

Beecham, Jenny and Hoadley, Ruth, *Techniques for Participation in Decision Making for Previously Uninvolved Groups*, School Community Interaction Trust, Victoria, 1980.

Parents' Rights and Responsibilities in Schools 1983. Report of public seminar, May 1983. Available from: Ms Helen Creed, Executive Officer, Community Taskforce, Education Department, 151 Royal Street, East Perth, WA, Australia, 6000.

Collection of short articles
8th Lorne Conference for Community Educators, A collection of short articles. Individual articles may be found in:
Educational Innovations 5, (1), 1979
- 'Ask a stupid question' (Mary Nicholas)
- 'Participation vs Involvement' (Hoadley, R. and Beacham, J.)
- 'Parents? Why Bother!' (Ted Poulton)
- 'Parents in Education — Sweden/Britain' (Gallagher)
- 'Definitions'

Racial Education Dossier 9, (Winter), 1979
- 'Community Involvement — Is Anything Really Happening?' (Robert Wilson)
- 'Popular Control in Education'

The School and Community: Community Centres Project, SA
- 'Problem Areas Where the School and Community Interact' (John Cusack)

School Bell, October, 1982
- 'Overseas Progress on Decision Making' (David Pettit)

Teachers and Parents No.1
- 'Children's Reading' (Victorian Federation of State Schools Parents Clubs)
- 'Charter of Parent Responsibilities, Rights' (A.C. S.S.O.)

Warden, J.W., *Citizen Participation — What Others Say — What Others Do.* Mid-Atlantic Centre for Community Education, Virginia, USA.

Short articles
'Alter Ego', 'The parent–teacher interview — battle cry or peace talk?' In *Inter View*, No.7, 1982. Education Department of Victoria.
A parent discusses some frustrating and rewarding experiences in parent–teacher interviews.

Cleary, Pauline, 'A Parent-involvement Kit', in *Study of Society*, November, 1981, Education Department of Victoria.
A description of the Northcote Community Parent Involvement Kit. The kit is partly a directory of names, addresses and telephone numbers, and partly a collection of practical ideas for teachers.

Hill, B.V., 'Community Involvement — A Practical Ideal?' in *The Educational Magazine*, Vol 36, No.5, 1979, Education Department of Victoria.

Hopkins, K., 'A Plus for Parent Involvement', in *The Educational Magazine*, Vol 39, No.4, 1982, Education Department of Victoria.

Shrimpton, Jan and Howat, Judy, 'The Gowerville Story: Parental Involvement in Developing a School Behaviour Policy', in *Inter View*, No.11, 1983, Education Department of Victoria.
Discusses the antecedents and planning of a productive meeting about school behaviour and discipline between parents and teachers of a primary school.

Ward, Stephen D., 'Parent–teacher interviews — objectives and some underlying problems', in *Inter View*, No.7, 1982, Education Department of

Resources

Victoria. This article seeks to clarify the purposes of parent-teacher interviews and discusses the following problems:
- Differing views on the aims of education
- Defensive manoeuvres by parents and teachers
- The use of jargon
- Parents' criticism of teachers not present in the interview
- How to get 'uninterested' parents to the school.

Films and videos

A Feeling of Self-worth, Monterey Primary School, Australia, 20 minutes.
   Film or video — for abstract see: School climate and organisation.

Closing the Gap: Changes from the Inside, Filmed for the Supplementary Grants Program, Education Department of Victoria.
   Video designed to help generate discussion about how to encourage parents to play a part in activities at your school. Filmed at an inner-city secondary school in a mixed ethnic community.

Parent Teacher Interviews, Australia, 1970, 28 minutes, colour
   Illustrates communication problems that can occur in parent-teacher interviews.

The All-purpose Parent Teacher Interview, Australia, 1978, 23 minutes, colour.
   How to conduct interviews to gain parents' interest and support for their children and for their school.

Student involvement and responsibility in school and community

Books

Boomer, Garth, *Negotiating the Curriculum: A teacher-student partnership*, Ashton Scholastic, Sydney, 1982.

Holt, John, *Freedom and Beyond*, Dutton, New York, 1972.

Kingston, Charles and Vozzo, Les, *The Hitch-hiker's Guide to Student Government: A Manual for Teachers*, West Wyalong High School/Australian Schools Commission Innovation Programs, 1982.

Booklet

Campbell, Elizabeth, *A Peer Support Program: Personal Development course for Secondary Schools*, 1982. Peer Support Foundation, c/- Elizabeth Campbell, 3-11 Addison Road, Manley, NSW, 2095.

Periodicals

Connect, Newsletter of the Youth Participation in Education Projects, 12 Brooke Street, Northcote, Victoria, Australia, 3070.

Resources For Youth, Newsletter of the National Commission on Resources for Youth Inc., 36 West 44th Street, New York, NY., USA, 10036.

Resources

Short Article
Kohler, Mary Conway, 'Developing Responsible Youth through Youth Participation', in *Phi Delta Kappan*, Feb., 1981, USA.

Kits
Lippitt, P., Eiseman, J.W., and Lippitt, R., *The Cross-age Helping Package* University of Michigan, Centre for Research on Utilization of Scientific Knowledge, 1969.
Kit contains a book, filmstrip and materials for training of teachers and of tutors. Available from Publications Division, Institution for Social Research, University of Michigan, PO Box 1248, Ann Arbor, Michigan, USA, 48108.

Mack, Glen and Les, *Why Not the Kids? Changes . . . from the inside*, G. and L. Mack, Glenn Mack Studio, 109 Kerferd Road, Albert Park, Victoria, Australia, 1984.
An 8-minute video showing interviews with students and a teacher from a primary school where students were given a say in making changes around the school. Kit also has stand-up display cards, question sheets (to assist in leading discussions) and return cards (for participants to record their ideas). Useful as a discussion starter.

Staff development and In-service training

See also the topic heading: Leadership and the process of change in schools.

Short articles
Brennan, Marie, 'Do-It-Yourself In-service: A New Look at Staff Meetings or Action Research for Staff Meetings', in *Idiom*, Autumn, 1982, Victorian Association for the teaching of English, Australia.
This article commends the action research framework as a practical approach to in-service and staff meetings.

Cumming, Jim, 'Days in our lives: making curriculum days more effective,' in *Viewpoints*, 1, 1984.
Gives valuable guidelines for making curriculum days more effective, particularly with regard to long-term outcomes of the activity.

Joyce, B. and Showers, B., 'Improving In-service Training: The Messages of Research,' in *Educational Leadership*, February, 1980.

McLaughlin, M.W. and Marsh, D.D., 'Staff Development and School Change', in *Teachers College Record*, Columbia University, 80, 1, September, 1978.

St Leger, Lawrence, 'What Makes a Professional Teacher,' in *Inter View*, No.3, 1981, Education Department of Victoria.
The author argues that an essential aspect of a professional staff is skill sharing or 'collegiate support and development'.

Resources

Curriculum and teaching methods as preventive approaches to discipline

Books

Boomer, Garth, *Negotiating the Curriculum: A teacher-student partnership*, Ashton Scholastic, Sydney, 1982.

Cohen, David and Harrison, Marelle, *Curriculum Action Project: A Report of Curriculum Decision-making in Australian Secondary Schools*, Curriculum Action Project, School of Education, Macquarie University, North Ryde, N.S.W., Australia, 2113.

Doll, Ronald C., *Curriculum Improvement: Decision Making and Process*, 5th ed, Allyn and Bacon, 1982.

Gnagney, W., 'Maintaining Discipline in Classroom Instruction', in *Current Topics in Classroom Instruction Series*, McMillan, New York, 1975.

Kounin, J., *Discipline and Group Management in Classrooms*, Holt, Rinehart and Winston, New York, 1970.

Booklet

Doyle, Walter, *Classroom Management*, Kappa Delta Pi, Indiana, 1980.

Short articles

Parry, Jo-Ann, 'A change for the better', in *Inter View*, No.4, 1981, Education Department of Victoria.
A description of curriculum innovations at Reservoir East Primary School. Some features are:
- a team approach to planning and training;
- weekly planning and evaluation meeting;
- students given some opportunity to select activities and to contribute to course evaluation.

Sparber, Ilona, 'Talking about classroom talk: Motivating children to learn', in *Inter View*, No.11, 1983, Education Department of Victoria.
Children become more involved in a topic and motivated to learn if they are encouraged to discuss the topic amongst themselves.

Tinney, Frank, 'Can't you get it right, just once!' in *Inter View*, No.1, 1980, Education Department of Victoria.
The teacher's most important task is to build on and maintain students' self confidence so that they believe they can attain skills through perseverance and practice.

Films and videos

Methods, Education Media, Hungary, 1970, Black and white, 22 minutes.
Film of three groups of kindergarten children. One is taught in an authoritarian style, one in a guided style and the third in a *laissez-faire* style. Based on Kurt Lewin's experiments.

Resources

Children with Special Abilities, Education Department of Victoria, 1984, 29 minutes.
   A film to stimulate discussion of curriculum strategies in the primary school. Filmed for the Gifted and Talented Children's Committee.

School climate and organisation

See also the topic headings: Leadership and the process of change in schools and Student welfare.

Books and reports

Fox, R.S. and others, *School Climate Improvement: A Challenge to the School Administrator*, Phi Delta Kappa, Indiana.

Fuller, Bruce and Lee, Girny, *Toward More Human Schools: Exemplary Efforts in Self-concept, Human Values, Parenting and School Climate*. A report to the California Legislature, California State Department of Education, Sacramento, 1981.

Lovegrove, T., Wilson, N., Teasedale, B. and Jackson, P., *Case Studies: Schools within Schools — Sub-schools in Australian Secondary Schools*, Education Department of South Australia, Flinders University, Relations, 1982.

Norman, Michael, *Woodleigh: An Alternative Design for Secondary Schooling*, Dove Communications, Victoria, Australia, 1982.

Robert, Marc, *Loneliness in the Schools*, Argus Communications, Illinois, 1974.

Robert, Marc, *School Morale: A human dimension*, Argus Communications, Illinois, 1976.

Rutter, M., Maughan, B., Mortimore, P. and Ouston, J., *Fifteen Thousand Hours: Secondary Schools and Their Effects on Children*, Open Books, London, 1979.

Wayson, W.W., *Developing Schools that Teach Self Discipline*, Ohio, 1980 (ED 196169).

Wayson, W.W., Devoss, G.G., Kaeser, S.C., Lasley, T. and Pinnell, G.S., *Handbook for Developing Schools with Good Discipline*, Phi Delta Kappa, Indiana, 1982.

Booklet

Hewitson, Mal, *The Hidden Curriculum: A Monograph*, Published by the author, 56 8th Avenue, St Lucia, Queensland, Australia, 4067, 1982.

Survey

Williams, Trevor and Batten, Margaret, *The Quality of School Life*, Australian Council for Educational Research, P.O. Box 210, Hawthorn, Vic., Australia, 3122, 1983.
   A description of the development of a model and measure of students' perceptions of the quality of their lives at school. (Authors' abstract.)

Resources

Short articles

Ann, Lisa and Robert, 'School Days: Are They the Most Sublime of Our Lives?' in *Inter View*, No.1, 1980, Education Department of Victoria.
Students discuss the kinds of behaviour they like and dislike in their teachers.

Breckenridge, Eileen, 'Improving School Climate', in *Phi Delta Kappan*, 58 (4), 1976.
A teacher describes the processes that took place to change a deteriorating school climate in just one year.

Drent, Ailsa, 'Dawn', in *Inter View*, No.6, 1982, Education Department of Victoria.
Story of a hearing-impaired girl who feared attending school. The article highlights a number of factors that helped to integrate Dawn into secondary school.

Hoey, Anne, 'Perspectives in listening', in *Inter View*, No.6, 1982, Education Department of Victoria.
Discusses the importance of teachers' listening to, and communicating warmth to students, and some aspects of teaching that make communication all the more difficult.

Maslow, A.J., 'A theory of human motivation', in *Human Dynamics in Psychology and Education*, Hamachek, D. (Ed.), Allyn and Bacon, Boston, 1972.

Maughan, Barbara and Ouston, Janet, 'Fifteen Thousand Hours: Findings and Implications', in *SET: Research Information for Teachers*, No.2, 1980, Item 7, NZCER and ACER.
Summarises results of a longitudinal research study in twelve secondary schools in a socially disadvantaged area of London. The main conclusions of this study are that some schools are more successful than others in promoting social and intellectual development and that many factors that influence the success of a school are within the power of teachers to shape and change.

McIntyre, Bev, 'Vandalism and the School', in *Inter View*, No.5, 1981, Education Department of Victoria.
Of interest here for its discussion of a range of strategies for prevention of vandalism.

Norman, Michael, 'The Woodleigh Way', in *Inter View*, No.9, 1983, Education Department of Victoria.
Woodleigh is a small private secondary school which differs from the more traditional school in a number of ways. For example:
• greater parent and student involvement in decision-making;
• 'homesteads' to cater for cross-age mini-schools or 'home groups';
• more varied curriculum — whilst retaining the traditional academic subjects;
• timetabling to allow for daily home group and elective activities and one week each term for a project in the community;

- students have more responsibility in the school (e.g. for construction, decorating, cleaning, canteen, school photographs).

Orzech, Susie, 'Welcome to Your Home Group', in *Inter View*, No.5, 1981, Education Department of Victoria.
 Cross-age home groups at Thomastown High School meet for four hours per week. Advantages for students stem both from interactions with a consistent group of students from all levels in the school and from contact with the home group teacher who is more like a friend and can offer counselling in personal and academic spheres.

St Leger, Lawrence, 'What Makes a Professional Teacher?' in *Inter View*, No.3, 1981, Education Department of Victoria.
 The author believes that an essential aspect of a professional staff is skill sharing or collegiate support and development.

Ward, Stephen D., 'Classroom Management', in *Inter View*, No.3, 1981, Education Department of Victoria.
 Discusses the relevance of the social environment and curriculum to classroom management and discipline.

Kit

Classroom Dynamics Part A: Discussion to accompany the video, *A new classroom — a study of classroom dynamics*, Equal Opportunity Unit, Education Department of Victoria.
 This kit looks at differences in the way teachers treat boys and girls. Available from Equal Opportunity Resource Centre, 29 Dawson Street, Brunswick, Victoria, Australia, 3056.

Films and videos

A Feeling of Self-worth, Monterey Primary School, Australia, 20 minutes.
 Video or film about Monterey Primary School. Could be used as a discussion starter on such issues as parent involvement in a school, curriculum improvement, integration of special programmes into the overall school system or ensuring some form of 'success' for all children.

I Taught Them but They Didn't Learn, Australia, 16 minutes.
 This film examines some cultural differences between teachers and students that can prevent students from performing well at school.

Maslow's Hierarchy of Need, Salenger Educational Media, 1975, 16 minutes.
 Presents Maslow's hierarchy of needs and gives work-force illustrations. Could be useful for stimulating discussion about either students' or teachers' needs.

Skipping Class, Trout Films, 1983.
 Film that could stimulate discussion on a variety of issues — e.g. communication between schools and parents, communication amongst school staff, careers guidance, cross-cultural communication.

Resources

Student welfare
Books
Rimmer, J., Pettit, D., Morgan, J. and Hodgson, J., *Schools and Welfare Work: An Evaluation of Innovative Program Models*, Department of Social Studies, University of Melbourne, 1984.

Short articles
Gilpin, Val, 'The Way I Feel', in *Inter View*, No.10, 1983, Education Department of Victoria.
   Illustrates some feelings of unhappy or depressed children and suggests ways in which a teacher might help.
Jenkin, Nettie, 'The Pupil Welfare Co-ordinator Scheme'.
Mrozik, Jean, 'Miss Grinton, here's your strap'.
Patford, Janet, 'Welfare Committees — a forum where schools can tackle the issues'.
Ward, Stephen, 'The teacher's role in welfare and guidance', all in *Inter View*, No.6, 1982, Education Department of Victoria.
   A series of articles which discusses both the nature of a welfare role for schools and teachers and a number of issues relating to this role. Curriculum, social organisation and the provision of guidance are all important aspects of student welfare.
Lopata, Rena, 'Do you have a Helen in your class?' in *Inter View*, No.4, 1981, Education Department of Victoria.
   There are frequent confrontations between Helen and her teachers. This is Helen's account of the situation, indicating some of her personal background and her feelings in response to the manner in which a number of teachers treat her.
Ochiltree, Gay, 'A challenge for teachers: Australian Children in Changing Families', in *Inter View*, No.11, 1983, Education Department of Victoria.
   Children and their parents can experience a variety of stresses when marriages break down and parents separate. Children may show emotional and social disturbances at these times and their school work may deteriorate. The article discusses these problems and indicates ways in which schools can help.
Pitman, Tony and Jukes, Ray, 'Coping with student stress at HSC', in *Inter View*, No.7, 1982, Education Department of Victoria.
   Gives some practical procedures teachers could follow if they are concerned about stress in their HSC students.

Interpersonal skills (for teachers)
See also under: Thomas Gordon and effectiveness training; and Assertion training for teachers.

Resources

Books

Egan, G., *The Skilled Helper: Models, Skills and Methods for Effective Helping*, 2nd Ed, Brooks Coles, California, 1982.

Egan, G., *Exercises in Helping Skills: A Training Manual to Accompany the Skilled Helper*, Revised Edition, Brooks Coles, Monterey, CA, 1981.

Gazda, G.M. and others, *Human Relations Development: A Manual for Educators*, 2nd Ed, Allyn and Bacon, Boston, 1977.

Ginnott, H.G., *Between Parent and Child: New Solutions to Old Problems*, New Edition, Staples Press, London, 1969.

Ginnott, H.G., *Teacher and Child*, McMillan, New York, 1971.

Ginnott, H.G., *Between Parent and Teenager*, Revised Edition, Cassell, London, 1973.

Johnston, D.W., *Reaching Out: Interpersonal Effectiveness and Self Actualisation*, Prentice Hall, Englewood Cliffs, N.J., 1972.

Long, L., *Listening/Responding: Human Relations Training for Teachers*, Brooks Cole, Monterey, CA., 1978.

Wittmer, J. and Myrick, R., *Facilitative Teaching Theory and Practice*. Goodyear Publishing Co., Pacific Palisades, C.S., 1974.

Films

What Do You Mean, What Do I Mean? Case Studies in Effective Communication, Salenger Educational Media, 1976, 18 minutes.
> The film illustrates two barriers to effective communication, (1) the way we see ourselves and (2) the way we see others. Aimed to help people be aware of the need for feedback and active listening.

As Others See Us, Salenger Educational Media, 1981, 10 minutes.
> Short film illustrating the Johari Window — a model for considering the effects of congruence or otherwise between the way people see themselves and the way other people see them.

Many Hear, Some Listen, Education Media, Australia, 1975, 10 minutes.
> A brief film indicating three barriers to accurate listening.

Nonverbal Communication, Salenger Educational Media, 1978, 17 minutes.
> The film's objective is to increase awareness and understanding of one's own and others' non-verbal messages.

Assertion training (for teachers)

Books

Alberti, R. and Emmons, M.L., *Your Perfect Right: A Guide to Assertive Behaviour*, 3rd Edition, Impact Publishing Company, California, 1978.

Bower, S.A. and Bower, G.A., *Asserting Yourself: A Practical Guide for Positive Change*, Addison Wesley, Reading Mass., 1976.

Fensterheim, H. and Baer, J., *Don't say 'yes' when you want to say 'no'*, Futura Publications, U.K., 1975.

Resources

Galassi, M. and Galassi, J.P. *Assert Yourself! How to be your own person*, Human Sciences Press, New York, 1977.

Self esteem, social skills training and values clarification (for students, although teachers may like to use some of the exercises for themselves)

Books

Baker, P. and Marshall, M.R., *More Simulation Games*, Joint Board of Christian Education of Australia and New Zealand, 1977.

Borba, Michele and Craig, *Self-esteem: A Classroom Affair: 101 ways to help children like themselves*, Winston Press, Minneapolis, 1978.

Camp, B.W. and Bash, M.A.S., *Think Aloud: Increasing Social and Cognitive Skills: A problem solving program for children*, Research Press, Illinois, 1981.

Canfield, J. and Wells, H., *100 Ways to Enhance Self-concept in the Classroom*, Prentice-Hall, New Jersey, 1976.

Cartledge, G. and Milburn, J.F., *Teaching Social Skills to Children: Innovative Approaches*, Pergamon, New York, 1980.

Chase, Larry, *The Other Side of the Report Card*, Goodyear, California, 1975.

Elaro, P. and Cooper, M., *Aware*, Addison-Wesley Publishing Co., London, 1977.

Goldstein, A.P. and Sprafkin, R.P., *Skill streaming and adolescent: A structured learning approach to prosocial skills*, Research press, Illinois, 1980.

Hendricks, G. and Wills, *The Centering Book*, Prentice Hall, USA, 1974.

Hendricks, G. and Roberts, T., *The Second Centering Book*, Prentice Hall, USA, 1977.

Howe, L.W. and Howe, M.M., *Personalizing Education: Values Clarification and Beyond*, Hart, New York, 1975.

Johnson, D.W., *Reaching Out: Interpersonal Effectiveness and Self Actualisation*, Prentice Hall, Englewood Cliffs, N.J., 1972.

Johnson, D.W. and Johnson, F.P., *Joining Together: Group Theory and Group Skills*, Prentice Hall, Englewood Cliffs, N.J., 1975.

Krupar, K., *Communication Games: Participants Manual*, Free Press, New York, 1973.

Lyon, H., *Learning To Feel, Feeling To Learn: Humanistic Education for the Whole Man*, Merrill, Ohio, 1971.

Miller, J.P., *Humanising the Classroom: Models of Teaching in Affective Education*, Praeger, New York, 1976.

Nielson, L., *How To Motivate Adolescents*, Prentice Hall, New York, 1983.

Pearson, K., *RAP Groups*, Youth Work Guides, Joint Board of Christian Education of Australia and New Zealand, 1975.

Pfeiffer, J.W., and Jones, J.E., *A Handbook of Structured Experiences for Human Relations Training*, Vol. 1-5, University Associates Press, Iowa City, 1969.

Resources

Raths, L.E., Harmin, M., and Simon, S., *Values and Teaching*, Charles E. Merrill Pub. Company, Ohio, 1966.

Reichert, R., *Self Awareness through Group Dynamics: Insights and Techniques for the Personal Growth of High School Students*, Pflaum, (Peter Li Inc.) Dayton, USA, 1970.

Rogers, C., *Freedom To Learn*, Charles E. Merrill, Columbus, Ohio, 1969.

Ruben, B.D. and Budd, R.W., *Human Communication Handbook*, Hayden, 1975.

Schrank, J., *Teaching Human Beings: 101 Subversive Games for the Classroom*, Beacon Press, Boston, 1972.

Schwartz, L., *Month to Month Me*, Learning Works, Santa Barbara, USA, 1976.

Simon, S., *Meeting Yourself Halfway*, Argus, Niles, Illinois, 1974.

Simon, S. and Clark, J., *Beginning Values Clarification*, Pennant Press, California, 1975.

Simon, S., Howe, L., and Kirschenbaum, H., *Values Clarification: A Handbook of Practical Strategies for Teachers and Students*, Hart Publishing Company, New York, 1972.

Simon, S., *I am loveable and capable*, Argus, Niles, Illinois, 1974.

Spence, S., *Social Skills Training with Children and Adolescents: A Counsellor's Manual*, London, NFER, 1980.

Spencer, G., King, A., and Donovan, L., *Where do you stand — A question of values*, Rigby Education, Melbourne, Australia, 1981.

Vernon, A., *Help Yourself to a Healthier You: A Handbook of Emotional Education Exercises for Children*, University Press of America, Lanham, 1980.

Resources guide

Focus on Self-development (teachers guide to workshops, tapes, film strips, pictures), Science Research Associates, Chicago.

Kits — Primary Level

Dinkmeyer, D. and Dinkmeyer, D. (Jr), *Developing Understanding of Self and Others*, D1 and D2 (DUSO), American Guidance Services, Minnesota, 1982.
Programmes of activities designed to help students' social and emotional development. D1 is for years 1-3 and D2 for years 3-5.

Dupont, H., Gardner, D., and Brody, D., *Towards Affective Development*, American Guidance Services, Circle Press, 1974.
Structured classroom lessons which are intended to aid affective development in primary school children.

Primary/Early Secondary Level

Reasoner, R.W., *Building Self-esteem*, Consulting Psychologists Press, California, 1982.
Kit contains an Administrator's Guide, Teachers' Guide and classroom materials and a Parents' Guide.

Resources

Secondary Level
Dupont, H. and Dupont, C., *Transition*, American Guidance Services, 1979.
> Programme to aid social and emotional development of 12-15 year old students.

Hopson, Barry and Scally, Mike, *Life Skills Teaching Programmes*, No.1 and 2, Lifeskills Associates, Ashling, Back Church Lane Leads, LS168DN, 1981.
> Teaching programmes in areas such as time management, interpersonal relationships, being assertive, finding a job.

Schwarzrock, S.P. and Wrenn, C.G. *Contemporary Concerns of Youth*, American Guidance Services, 1979.
> Materials for use in discussion and problem solving activities designed to promote social development.

School rules
Short article
McDaniel, T., 'Well Begun Is Half Done! A School-wide Project for Better Discipline', in *SET: Research Information for Teachers*, 1982, No.1, Item 9, NZCER and ACER.
> For abstract, see Leadership and the Process of Change in Schools.

Kit
Reasoner, R.W., *Building Self-esteem*, Consulting Psychologists Press, California, 1982.
> This kit has a series of lesson plans for opening up discussion about rules, rights and responsibilities at school and at home.

Examples of school rules
Yarra Junction Primary School, *The Golden Rules*.
> A pleasantly worded and most imaginatively illustrated set of rules. Copies can be obtained at a small cost from Yarra Junction Primary School.

Behaviour management: resources covering a range of models
Books
Charles, C.M., *Building Classroom Discipline: From Models to Practice*, Longman, New York and London, 1981.

Keuss, Jeffrey F., *Positive Discipline Techniques*, Order from: Bendigo Education Centre, PO Box 442, Havlin Street, Bendigo, Australia, 3550.

Sprick, R., *Solutions Book: A Guide to Classroom Discipline*, Science Research Associates, Chicago, 1981.

Sutton, G. and Cruickshank, B., *HELP, They Are Eliminating Corporal Punishment: A Discipline Resource Manual*, 1983. Available from: Swan

Resources

Hill Curriculum Services Centre, 210 Beveridge Street, Swan Hill, Victoria, Australia.

Wolfgang, G. and Glickman, C., *Solving Discipline Problems: Strategies for Classroom Teachers*, Allyn and Bacon, Boston, 1980.

Workshop notes
Hyman, I. and others, *Seven Approaches to Discipline: Workshop Notes*, National Centre for the Study of Corporal Punishment and Alternatives in the Schools, 833 Ritter Hall South, Philadelphia, Pennsylvania, USA, 19122.

Short article
McDaniel, T., 'Exploring alternatives to punishment: the keys to effective discipline', in *Phi Delta Kappan*, 1980, 61, (7).

Kit
Discipline! Where Do You Stand? Institute of Educational Administration, Geelong, Australia, 1984.

The kit contains five units, each with an audio-tape and printed notes. Unit 1 is based on the material in this book.
Unit 1: Setting up a discipline policy
Unit 2: Reinforcement theory
Unit 3: Individual psychology
Unit 4: The Glasser system
Unit 5: Theoretical perspectives.

Behaviour management:
Assertive models
Books
Canter, L. and Canter, M., *Assertive Discipline: A Take-charge Approach for Today's Educator*, Canter and Associates, California, 1976.

Dobson, J., *Dare to Discipline*, Kingsway Publications, Great Britain, 1975.

Gnagney, William J., *Motivating Classroom Discipline*, McMillan, New York, 1981.

Silberman, M.L. and Wheelan, S.A., *How to discipline without feeling guilty: Assertive relationships with children*, Research Press, Illinois, 1980.

Behaviour management:
Behaviour modification
Books for teachers
Axelrod, S., *Behaviour Modification for the Classroom teacher*, McGraw-Hill, New York, 1977.

Resources

Becker, W., Engelman, S. and Thomas, D., *Teaching I — Classroom Management* Science Research Associates, Chicago, 1975.

Blackman, G., Silberman, A., *Modification of Child and Adolescent Behaviour*, Wadsworth, Belmont, 1980.

Books for parents

Hofmeister, Alan M., Atkinson, Charles and Henderson, Hester, *What Do I Do Now? Practical Ways to Develop Good Behaviour in Your Child*, Argus Communications, Illinois, 1978.

Patterson, G.R. and Gullion, M.E., *Living with Children, New Methods for Parents and Teachers*, Research Press, Champaign, Illinois, 1971.

Sloane, H., *Stop that Fighting, Dinner's Ready, Not Till Your Room's Clean, No More Whining, Because I Said So*, How To Publications, California, 1976.

Short articles

Amey, Terry, 'Can I Enjoy My Teaching More?' in *Inter View*, No.1, 1980. Education Department of Victoria.
An introduction to the basic principles of behaviour modification theory. Gives examples of how specific classroom behaviours might be changed.

Cullen, Maureen and Wilks, Ray with Baker, Leanne, 'Fly me to the moon', in *Inter View*, No.1, 1980, Education Department of Victoria.
Describes a behaviour modification 'game' used with a class of third grade primary students.

Jacobs, Neil, 'Grandma's Law in the Classroom', in *Inter View*, No. 1, 1980, Education Department of Victoria.
Discusses the commonsense principle that popular activities can be used to encourage unpopular ones, e.g. 'Pack up the sports equipment and then you can go to lunch'.

McCarthy, Peter, Freeman, Liz, Rothwell, Chris, and Arnheim, Barbara, 'Is there life after 8D?' in *Inter View*, No.11, 1983, Education Department of Victoria.
Two examples of success in using group reinforcement at the post-primary level.

Walsh, Des, 'Behaviour Modification for Citizens and Academicians'. SET 77, No.2, Item 4, NZCER and ACER.

Wilks, Ray, 'When the carrot has been eaten, then what?' in *Inter View*, No. 3, 1981, Education Department of Victoria.
Discusses how to maintain a behaviour change that may have been brought about using artificial or token rewards.

Kit

Barnes, Colin and others, Reinforcement Theory: Unit 2 from *Discipline! Where Do You Stand?* Institute of Educational Administration, Geelong, Australia, 1984.
Kit includes an audio-tape and text about behaviour modification.

Behaviour management:
Cognitive behaviour modification and Rational Emotive Therapy

Books
Bernard, M.E. and Joyce, M.R., *Applying Rational-emotive Therapy with Children and Adolescents*, Wiley, New York, 1983.

Ellis, A. and Bernard, M., *Rational Emotive Approaches to the Problems of Childhood*, Plenum Press, New York, 1984.

Ellis, A. and Harper, R., *A New Guide to Rational Living*, Wiltshire Book Company, California, 1978.

Workman, E.A., *Teaching Behavioural Self Control to Students*, Pro-Ed, Austin, Texas, 1982.

Behaviour management:
Glasser's Reality Therapy approach

Books
Glasser, Naomi (Ed.) with introduction by William Glasser, *What Are You doing? How People Are Helped through Reality Therapy*, Harper and Row, New York, 1980.

Glasser, W., *Reality Therapy: A New Approach to Psychiatry*, Harper and Row, New York, 1965.

Glasser, W., *Schools without Failure*, Harper and Row, New York, 1969.

Glasser, W., *The Identity Society*, Harper and Row, New York, 1972.

Glasser, W., *Positive Addiction*, Harper and Row, New York, 1972.

Glasser, W., *Stations of the Mind. New Direction for Reality Therapy*. Harper and Row, New York, 1981.

Short articles
Freeman, Liz., 'Bandwagons and How Not To Fall Off: Cautionary Tales about Glasser's Reality Therapy', in *Inter View*, No.11, 1983, Education Department of Victoria.
  A discussion of problems that can emerge as schools begin to implement Glasser's ideas. Emphasises the need for schools to make a complete study of Glasser's concepts and to commit themselves to an extended period of policy and professional development.

Glasser, W., 'Disorders in Our Schools: Causes and Remedies', in *Phi Delta Kappan*, Jan., 1978.
  Glasser argues that the key to better discipline is to give students a stake in the school, to care for them and to teach them without failure. Punishment is not likely to be effective.

Resources

Glasser, W., edited by Hutchinson, J.L., 'A Ten Step Program' in *Educare Journal*, Spring, 1976, University of South Africa, Pretoria.

Glasser, W., 'Ten Steps to Good Discipline', in *Today's Education*, 66, (4), 1971, National Education Association, USA.
  An outline of Glasser's ten step discipline programme for schools.

Glasser, W., 'Failure at School — Its Effects', *National Elementary Principal*, Sept. 1969, Arlington, V.A.
  Glasser attributes much delinquent or withdrawn behaviour in students to a school's grading (and hence failing) policies. To break out of this cycle schools need to help students establish a success identity. They can do this by convincing the students that they are cared for and that they can achieve something worthwhile in school. The article also gives some guidelines for responding to misbehaviour when it does occur.

Glasser, W., 'Glasser's Reality Therapy for the Teacher', in *Inter View*, No. 8, 1983.
  One-page summary of the eight steps of Reality Therapy.

McCarthy, P., 'Classroom Meetings', in *Inter View*, No.10, 1983, Education Department of Victoria.
  An abridged version appears in this book.

Rand, M., 'The Reality of Glasser's Therapy: An integrated welfare approach to school discipline', in *Inter View*, No.4, 1981, Education Department of Victoria.
  Kerang Technical/High School is a pleasant place to be. The discipline policy at this school is based on the Glasser system. The article includes, but is not confined to, Glasser's ten steps.

Rand, M., 'Reality Therapy and Education: Simple but not easy', in *Inter View*, No.8, 1983, Education Department of Victoria.
  School experiences with the Glasser's ten step system of discipline.

Ward, S., 'A Hec of a Lot of Help', in *Inter View*, No.2, 1980, Education Department of Victoria.
  Story of how a teacher manages to help a student who is unpopular with both peers and teachers.

Ward, S., Contracting as Part of the Teacher-Student Problem Solving Process, in *Inter View*, No.8, 1983, Education Department of Victoria.
  Further discussion of conflict resolution and contracting between teachers and students.

Kit

Clarke, K. and Freeman, L., The Glasser System. Unit 4 from *Discipline! Where Do You Stand?* Institute of Educational Administration, Geelong, Australia, 1984.
  The kit includes an audio-tape and text describing the Glasser system.

Films*

Ten Step Discipline Program.
> Film of a lecture by Dr Glasser.

How To Use Reality Therapy in the Classroom.
> Film of a panel discussion in which Glasser discusses how teachers can use his eight steps of Reality Therapy to work with students experiencing problems.

Reality Therapy 1: Personal Strength and Success Identity.
> People who have a positive self-image will act in a more rational and socially acceptable way.

Reality Therapy 2: Dealing with Effects of Failure Identity.
> Dr Glasser gives some insight into the behaviour of failing people and some down-to-earth suggestions for stopping and reversing their negative behaviour.

Positive School Climate: Creating an Atmosphere for Effective Discipline.
> Dr Glasser discusses the schools without failure concepts. Effective discipline takes place in an environment in which people care for and respect each other and in which students are motivated to learn.

Strengthening Today's Children.
> Ideas to help parents improve the quality of family life.

Reality Therapy and Discipline at Home.
> Dr Glasser presents the basic steps of reality therapy and shows how each step is applied in a parent-child situation.

Improving Family Relationships.
> Companion film to *Reality Therapy and Discipline at home.* Dr Glasser answers questions about reality therapy and its application in the home.

Positive Addiction, an Alternative to Drugs.
> Advice for parents relating to kids' use of drugs. Also discusses negative effects on children of watching too much television.

* Australian Distributors of Glasser films: Trigger Visuals, 150 Concord Road, North Strathfield, NSW, Australia, 2137.

Behaviour Management:
Dreikurs and Systematic Training for Effective Teaching

Books

Balson, M., *Becoming Better Parents*, ACER, Melbourne, 1981.

Balson, M., *Understanding Classroom Behaviour*, ACER, Melbourne, 1982.

Baruth, L. and Eckstein, D., *The ABCs of Classroom Discipline*, Kendal/Hunt, Dubuque, 1A, 1976.

Dreikurs, R., *Psychology in the Classroom*, 2nd Edition, Harper and Row, New York, 1968.

Dreikurs, R. and Cassel, P., *Discipline Without Tears*, Hawthorn Books, New York, 1972.

Resources

Dreikurs, R., Grunwald, B. and Pepper. F., *Maintaining Sanity in the Classroom*. 2nd Edition, Harper and Row, New York, 1980.

Dreikurs, R. and Soltz, V., *Happy Children: A Challenge to Parents*, Fontana, Great Britain, 1972.

Short articles

Tinney, Frank., 'Can't you get it right, just once!' in *Inter View*, No.1, 1980, Education Department of Victoria.
For abstract, see: Curriculum and teaching methods as preventive approaches to discipline, in this bibliography.

Kits*

Dinkmeyer, D. and McKay, G.D., *Systematic Training for Effective Parenting*, American Guidance Services, USA, 1982.
Kits contain audio-cassettes, charts, leaders guide and parents handbook.

Dinkmeyer, D. McKay, G.D., and Dinkmeyer, D. (Jr.) *Systematic Training for Effective Teaching*, American Guidance Services, USA, 1980.
Kit contains a Teacher's Handbook, Teacher's Resource Book, Leaders' Manual, audio-cassettes and charts.

Dinkmeyer, D. and McKay, G.D., *STEP/Teen Systematic Training for Effective Parenting of Teens*, American Guidance Services, USA, 1983.
Kit includes a Parents' Guide, Leader's Guide, audio-cassettes, charts and posters.

* There are no special qualifications required to lead the *Systematic Training* courses.

Behaviour management:
Thomas Gordon and Teacher Effectiveness Training

Books

Gordon, Thomas, *P.E.T.: Parent Effectiveness Training*, New American Library, New York, 1975.

Gordon, Thomas, with Burch, Noel, *T.E.T.: Teacher Effectiveness Training*, Peter H. Wyden, New York, 1974.

Gordon, Thomas, with Gordon-Sands, Judith, *P.E.T. in Action: New Problems, Insights and Solutions in Parent Effectiveness Training*, Wyden Books, United States and Canada, 1976.

Short article

Freeman, L., Hont, G., and McCarthy, P., 'I'd like to see you after class, Jo . . .' in *Inter View*, No.8, 1983, Education Department of Victoria. Discusses the way teachers can use Thomas Gordon's No-lose Method of problem solving and conflict resolution to work through problems with students.

Behaviour Management:
Transactional Analysis
Books
Berne, Eric, *Games People Play: The Psychology of Human Relationships*, Grove, New York, 1967.
Ernst, Ken, *Games Students Play and What To Do About Them*, Celestial Arts, California, 1973.
Freed, A.M., *T.A. for Teens*, Jalmar Press, Sacramento, 1976.
Freed, A.M., *T.A. for Kids (and Grown-Ups Too)*, Jalmar Press, Sacramento, 1971.
Freed, A.M., *T.A. for Tots (and other Princes)*, Jalmar Press, Sacramento, 1973.
Harris, T., *'I'm O.K.–You're O.K.': A Practical Guide to Transactional Analysis*, Harper and Row, New York, 1969.

Films*
Games We Play in High School, 29 minutes.
> Discusses how transactional analysis concepts can be used to help improve relationships, learning and discipline in secondary schools.

The OK Classroom, 29 minutes.
> Introduces the concepts of transactional analysis and gives examples of the theory in action.

* Both available from: Media Five, 3211 Cahuenga Boulevard West, Lost Angeles, California. 90068.

Additional Resources for the Revised Edition:
Books
Balson, M., *Understanding Classroom Behaviour*, 2nd Ed., Australian Council for Educational Research, Hawthorn, Victoria, 1988.
Blachford, Peter, *Playtime in the Primary School: Problems and Improvements*, NFER-Nelson, Windsor, England, 1989.
Bolton, R., *People Skills: How to Assert Yourself, Listen to Others, and Resolve Conflicts*, Prentice-Hall of Australia, Sydney, 1986.
Bull, Shirley L. and Solity, Jonathon E., *Classroom Management: Principles to Practice*, Croom Helm, London, 1987.
Caldwell, Brian J. and Spinks, Jim M., *The Self-Managing School*, The Falmer Press, East Sussex, 1988.
Canter, Lee, *Assertive Discipline: Administrator Guide*, Canter and Associates, Santa Monica, California, 1986.
Canter, Lee with Canter, Marlene, *Assertive Discipline: Resource Materials Workbook, Elementary (Grades K-6)*. Revised Ed., Canter and Associates, Santa Monica, California, 1984.

Resources

Canter, Lee with Canter, Marlene, *Assertive Discipline: Resource Materials Workbook, Secondary (Grades 7-12).* Revised Ed., Canter and Associates, Santa Monica, California, 1984.

Canter, Lee and Canter, Marlene, *Assertive Discipline: Phase 2 Teacher Workbook, K-12,* Canter and Associates, Santa Monica, California, 1986.

Carter, F. and Cheesman, P., *Anxiety in Childhood and Adolescence; Encouraging Self-Help Through Relaxation Training,* Croom Helm, Kent, U.K., 1988.

Carter, Mildred, *Effective School Discipline Through Democratic Participation.* Fastback Series No. 250, Phi Delta Kappa Educational Foundation, 1987.

Clemett, Anthony J. and Pearce, John S., *The Evaluation of Pastoral Care,* Basil Blackwell, Oxford, 1986.

Cornelius H. and Faire, S., *Everyone Can Win: How to Resolve Conflict,* Simon and Schuster, Australia, Brookvale, N.S.W., 1989.

Charles, C.M., *Building Classroom Discipline: From Models to Practice.* 3rd. Ed., Longman, New York, 1989.

Curran, Dolores, *Working With Parents: Dolores Curran's Guide to Successful Parent Groups,* American Guidance Service, Minnesota, 1989.

Drent, Ailsa, *Parenting Today: Discipline Partnerships Between Home and School.* Australian Council for Educational Research, Hawthorn, Vic., 1990.

Egan, G., *Change Agent Skills in Helping and Human Services Settings,* Brooks/Cole, Monterey, California, 1985.

Egan, G., *Exercises in Helping Skills: A Training Manual to Accompany the Skilled Helper,* 3rd Ed., Brooks/Cole, California, 1985.

Egan, Gerard, *The Skilled Helper: A Systematic Model for Helping,* Brooks/Cole, California, 1986.

Egan, G. and Cowan, M., *People in Systems,* Brooks/Cole, California, 1985.

Evertson, C.M., Emmer, E.T., Clements, B.S., Sanford, J.P. and Worsham, M.E., *Classroom Management for Elementary Teachers,* 2nd Ed., Prentice Hall, Englewood Cliffs, New Jersey, 1989.

Feindler, Eva L. and Ecton, Randolph B., *Adolescent Anger Control: Cognitive Behavioural Techniques,* Pergamon Press, New York, 1986.

Feuerstein, M., *Partners in Evaluation; Evaluating Development and Community Programmes with Participants,* Macmillan, London, 1986.

Fontana, David, *Classroom Control: Psychology in Action,* The British Psychological Society and Metheun, London, 1987.

Glasser, W. *Control Theory,* Harper and Row, New York, 1985.

Glasser, W., *Control Theory in the Classroom,* Harper and Row, New York, 1986.

Geldard, D., *Basic Personal Counselling: A Training Manual for Counsellors,* Prentice-Hall, Australia, 1989.

Resources

Goldstein, Arnold P. and Keller, Harold, *Aggressive Behaviour Assessment and Intervention,* Pergamon Press, New York, 1987.

Grunsell, Rob, *Finding Answers to Disruption: Discussion Exercises for Secondary Teachers,* Longman, York, 1985.

Hall, G.E. and Hord, S.M., *Change in Schools,* State University of New York Press, New York, 1987.

Hopes, C. (Ed)., *The School Leader and School Improvement,* ACCO, Leuven, 1986.

Hord, S.M., *Evaluating Educational Innovation,* Croom Helm, Sydney, 1987.

Kotzman, Anne, *Listen to Me, Listen to You: A Practical Guide to Improving Self-esteem, Listening Skills and Assertiveness,* Penguin Books, Australia, 1989.

Lewis, R., *The Classroom Discipline Dilemma: Direction, Influence or Control,* Australian Council for Educational Research, Hawthorn, Victoria, in press.

Lewis, Ramon and Lewis, Susan, *The Parenting Puzzle,* Australian Council for Educational Research, Hawthorn, Victoria, 1989.

Lewis, Ramon and Lovegrove, Malcolm, (Eds.), *Best of Set: Discipline,* Australian Council for Educational Research, Hawthorn, Victoria, 1989.

Lovegrove, Malcolm N., Lewis, Ramon and Burman, Eva, *You Can't Make Me! Developing Effective Classroom Discipline,* Latrobe University Press, Melbourne, Australia, 1989.

Mann, Leon, Harmoni, Ros and Power, Colin, *GOFER: Decision Making in Practice.* The Flinders University Decision Course for Schools, Curriculum Development Centre, (PO Box 34, Woden, ACT, Australia, 2606), 1988.

Marsh, C., *Spotlight on School Improvement,* Allen and Unwin, London, 1988.

McCrae, D., *Teachers, Schools and Change,* Heinemann Educational Australia in Association with the Curriculum Development Centre, Woden A.C.T., 1988.

McGregor, Robert, *Working Together: The Co-operative English Classroom,* Nelson, Melbourne, Australia, 1989.

Mearns, D. and Thorne, B., *Person-centred Counselling in Action,* Sage, Beverley Hills, 1988.

Montgomery, Bob, *Working Together: A Practical Guide to Collaborative Decision Making,* Nelson, Melbourne, Australia, 1986. (Available from: Applied Behaviour Research Associates, 3 Alexandra Pde., Collingwood, Victoria, Australia, 3066. Tel. 03 416 1278. Ask for their catalogue of self-help books and tapes.)

Montgomery, Bob and Evans, Lynette *You and Stress: A Guide to Successful Living,* Nelson, Melbourne, Australia, 1984.

Montgomery, Bob and Morris, Laurel, *Getting On With Your Teenagers: Bridging the Generation Gap,* Lothian, Port Melbourne, Australia, 1988.

Montgomery, Bob and Morris, Laurel, *Getting On With the Oldies, Bridging the Generation Gap,* Lothian, Port Melbourne, Australia, 1988.

Resources

Montgomery, Diane, *Managing Behaviour Problems*, Hodder and Stoughton, London, 1989.

Murphy L., *A Framework for Positive Approaches to Students' Behaviour*, Education Department of Tasmania, Hobart, 1986.

Nelson-Jones, Richard, *Practical Counselling and Helping Skills*, 2nd Ed., Holt, Rinehart and Winston, Marrickville, N.S.W., Australia, 1988.

Nelson-Jones, Richard, *Thinking Skills: Managing and Preventing Personal Problems*, Thomas Nelson, Melbourne, Australia, 1990.

Organisation for Economic Co-operation and Development, *Schools and Quality, an International Report*. Reproduced by the Australian Commonwealth Department of Employment, Education and Training, Canberra, 1989.

Osborn, D. Keith and Osborn, Janie D., *Discipline and Classroom Management*, 3rd Ed., Daye Press, 1989.

Otto, Rosemarie, *Teachers Under Stress; Health Hazards in a Work-role and Modes of Response*, Hill of Content Pub. Co., Melbourne, Australia, 1986.

Pope, A.W., McHale, S.M. and Craighead, W.E., *Self-Esteem Enhancement with Children and Adolescents*, Pergamon Press, NY, U.S.A., 1988.

Rogers, William A., *Making a Discipline Plan: Developing Classroom Management Skills*, Thomas Nelson, Melbourne, Australia, 1989.

Sandoval, J. (Ed.), *Crisis Counselling, Intervention and Prevention in the Schools*, Lawrence Erlbaum Associates, Hillsdale, New Jersey, 1988.

Scott, Sharon, *Peer Pressure Reversal, An Adult Guide to Developing a Responsible Child*, Human Resource Development Press, Amherst, MA, 1985.*

Scott, S., *How to Say No and Keep Your Friends, Peer Pressure Reversal for Teens and Preteens*, H.R.D.P., Amherst, MA, 1986.*

Scott, S., *Positive Peer Groups*, H.R.D.P., Amherst, MA, 1988.*

Scott, S., *When to Say Yes! and Make More Friends*, H.R.D.P., Amherst, MA, 1988*

Slee, Roger (Ed), *Discipline and Schools, a Curriculum Perspective*, Macmillan, Australia, 1988.

Sprick, Randall S., *The Solution Book: A Guide to Class Discipline*, Science Research Associates, 1988.

Tattum, Delwyn P. and Lane, David A. (Eds), *Bullying in Schools*, Trentham Books, Stoke-on-Trent, 1989.

Topping, Keith, *Educational Systems for Disruptive Adolescents*, Croom Helm; Reprinted 1987.

Victorian Branch of the Australian Psychological Society, *Psychology and You, Articles on Behaviour, Education, Health, Family and Society*, Artmenis, Hobart, Tasmania, 1989. ('Psych. & You', PO Box 238, Boronia, Vic. 3155).

Watkins, Chris and Wagner, Patsy, *School Discipline: A Whole-School Practical Approach*, Basil Blackwell, Oxford, 1987.

* Human Resource Development Press, 22 Amherst Rd., Amherst, MA, USA, 01002.

Wheldall, Kevin, and Glynn, Ted., *Effective Classroom Learning*, Basil Blackwell, 1989.
Wolfgang, C.H. and Glickman, C.D., *Solving Discipline Problems*, 2nd Ed., Allyn and Bacon, Boston, Massachusetts, 1986.
Wragg, Jeffrey, *Talk Sense to Yourself: A Program for Children and Adolescents*, Australian Council for Educational Research, Hawthorn, Victoria, 1989.

Annotated Bibliographies

Gray, Libby, *Select Reading Lists: 1. School Based Evaluation, 4. Stress, 1983, 13. Discipline Policy, 1985, 16. Discipline: Some Issues and Problems, 17. Discipline: Classroom Management, 1985, 19. Participative Decision Making, 1986*, Education Department Library Service, G.P.O. Box 4367, Melbourne, Australia, 3001. (Tel. 03 628 2464).
Karnes, Elizabeth L., Black, Donald D. and Downs, John L. (Eds), *Discipline in Our Schools: An Annotated Bibliography*, Greenwood Press, London, 1984.

Short Articles

ACT Schools Authority, *A Study of Discipline Policies and Practices in ACT Government Schools; Summary*, ACT Schools Authority, Canberra, 1986. (ACT Schools Authority, PO Box 20, Civic Square, ACT, Australia, 2608).
Amatea, Ellen S., *Brief systemic intervention with school behaviour problems: a case of temper tantrums*, Psychology in the Schools 25: 174-83, Ap 1988.
Armstrong G., *Discipline: How Can We Help the Teacher Who's Failing?* Practising Administrator, 9 No. 3: 32-34, 1987.
Ban, John R., *A Systems Approach to School Discipline*, The Education Digest, 51: 32-5 Mr 1986.
Ban, John R., *Discipline Literacy for Parents: an Imperative for the Eighties*, NASSP Bulletin 71: 111-15 Mr 1987.
Balson, M., *Understanding and Preventing Behavioural Problems in Schools*, Practising Administrator 10 2:34-39 1988.
Bartlett, Larry, *Academic evaluation and student discipline don't mix: a critical review*, Journal of Law and Education 16: 155-65 Spr 1987.
Bernard, Michael, *Classroom discipline and the effective self-management of teacher stress*, Set: Research Information for Teachers, No. 2, 1988.
Brophy, Jere, *Educating Teachers About Managing Classrooms and Students*, Teaching and Teacher Education 4 1: 1-18 1988.
Brown, William and Payne, Tyrone, *Policies/Practices in Public School Discipline*, Academic Therapy 23: 297-301 Ja 1988.
Brown, William and Payne, Tyrone, *Discipline In-service Training in the Public School: Teacher Responses and a Proposed Model*, Education (Chula Vista, Calif.) 108: 511-15 Summ 1988.
Brown, William and Payne, Tyrone, *Changes in School Discipline: For Better or Worse?* The Education Digest 54: 34-5 S 1988.

Resources

Canter, Lee, *You Can Get Home and School Working Together on Discipline Problems*, Thrust (Burlingame, Calif.) 13: 27-9 S 1983.

Carter, Mildred, *A Model for Effective School Discipline* (at Prospect School), Phi Delta Kappa Fastbacks 250: 7-34 1987.

Cohen, B., *Punishment Styles, a Guide to School's Value System*, Age, p20, 9 Aug. 1988. (Newspaper, Melbourne, Australia).

Cornell, Nancy, *Encouraging Responsibility — a Discipline Plan That Works*, Learning 86 15: 46-9 S 1986.

Cullingford, Cedric, *School Rules and Children's Attitudes to Discipline*, Educational Research 30: 3-8 F 1988.

Ewashen, George, Harris, Steven and Porter, Donna, *School Suspension Alternatives* (Behaviour Intervention Centre in Calgary, Canada), Education Canada 28: 4-9 Spr 1988.

Deering, Raymond P., *Discipline: Dealing with Emotions*, NASSP Bulletin 72: 105-6 F 1988.

Dobson J. and Gale R., *Corporal Punishment: Help for Teachers*, Set No. 1, 1985.

Dubelle, Stanley T. and Hoffman, Carol M. *When an attention-seeker gets under your skin* (excerpts from Misbehavin': solving the disciplinary puzzle for educators) Principal (Reston, Va.) 66: 28-30 Mr 1987.

Duke, Danial L. and Jones, Vernon F., *Two Decades of Discipline — Assessing the Development of an Educational Specialization*, Journal of Research and Development in Education 17: 25-35 Summ 1984.

Fischel, Frank J., *In-school Suspension Programs — Questions to Consider*, NASSP Bulletin 70: 100-2 N 1986.

Georgiady, Nicholas P. and Lazares, John, *Parents Help Deter Discipline Problems*, NASSP Bulletin 71: 133-4 D 1987.

Greene, Brad and Uroff, Shayle, *Increasing Student Achievement Through Increased Self-esteem*, Thrust (Burlingame, Calif.) 18: 40-2 F/Mr 1989.

Gill, Walter and Hayes-Butler, Karen, *Using Role Play and Video Technology in Building Schoolwide Discipline Programs*, Education (Chula Vista, Calif.) 109: 196-9 Wint 1988.

Harrison-Mattley P., *Discipline, Teacher Stress and the Quality of Education*, ACES Review 12 1: 1-3 1985.

Huber, Joseph D., *Discipline in the Middle School — Parent, Teacher and Principal Concerns*, NASSP Bulletin 68: 74-9 Ap 1984.

Huff, Joseph A., *Personalized Behavior Modification: An In-school Suspension Program that Teaches Students How to Change*, The School Counselor 35: 210-14 Ja 1988.

Hyman, Irwin A. and D'Alessandro, John, *Oversimplifying the School Discipline Problem*, The Education Digest 50: 18-20 N 1984.

Hyman, Irwin A. and D'Alessandro, John, *Good, Old-fashioned Discipline: the Politics of Punitiveness*, Phi Delta Kappa 66: 39-45 S 1984.

Johnston, Joanne S., *In-school Suspension from the Students' Perspective*, NASSP Bulletin 71: 122-4+ S 1987.

Resources

Lawrence, Jean, *Whipping post* (pupils' letters to the Elton inquiry), The Times Educational Supplement 3754: 25 Je 10 1988.

Lawrence, Jean, Steed, D.M. and Young, P., *European Voices on Disruptive Behaviour in Schools; Definitions, Concern, and Types of Behaviour*, British Journal of Educational Studies 32: 4-17 F 1984.

Lovegrove, M.N., Lewis, R., Fall C. and Lovegrove H., *Students' Preferences for Discipline Practices in Schools*, Teaching and Teacher Education (US) 1 No 4: 325-333 1985.

Maxwell, William, *What Teachers Think of Discipline After the Belt*, Times Educational Supplement Scotland, 1068: p2 Apr 24 1987.

Major, Robert L., *Discipline: the Most Important Subject We Teach*, NASSP Bulletin 72: 106-7 F 1988.

McCormack, Sammie, *Implementing an Effective Discipline Program*, Thrust (Burlingame, Calif.) 18: 43-4 F/Mr 1989.

McClean, Alan, *After the Belt: School Processes in Low-exclusion Schools*, School Organization, 7 No. 3: 303-310 Sep-Dec 1987.

McFadden, J., *Bullies and Victims: Strategies for Teachers*, Primary Education 17 No. 5: 24-26 1986.

McNergney, Robert and Haberman, Martin, *Research on Teaching: Teaching Aggressive Children*, Educational leadership 45: 96 D 1987/Ja 1988.

Melton, Keith and Long, Martin, *Alias Smith and Jones*, (contract behavior program at King's Lynn School, Norfolk, England), The Times Educational Supplement 3641: 23 Ap 11 1986.

Merret, Frank and Wheldall, Kevin, *Case Studies in Positive Teaching, II: More Examples Showing Behavioural Strategies in Action at the Secondary Level*, Behavioural Approaches with Children 12 No. 1: 25-35, 1988.

Nicholson, George Stephens and Ronald Elder, Rory, *Safe Schools: You Can't do it Alone*, Phi Delta Kappan 66: 491-6 Mr 1985.

Olweus, Dan, *Bullying in the Schools: How Educators can Help*, The Education Digest 53: 30-4 Mr 1988.

Owner, A., *Class Meetings: Part of a Systems' Approach to the Management of Difficult Children*, Behaviour Problems Bulletin 2 No. 2: 30-32 May 1988.

Petti, Michael, *Help for the Hot-tempered Kid*, Instructor (New York, N.Y.) 95: 56-7+ Mr 1986.

Schloss, Patrick J. and Maxymuik, Anna, *Discipline Articles in Educational Journals: is Empirical Work Keeping Pace with professional Interest?* Education (Chula Vista, Calif.) 106: 62-6 Fall 1985.

Short, Paula M. and Short, Rick Jay, *Beyond Technique: Personal and Organizational Influences on School Discipline*, The High School Journal 71: 31-6 O/N 1987.

Slacken, D.M., *Due Process and Democracy: Participation in School Disciplinary Processes*, Urban Education 23: 323-47 Ja 1989.

Resources

Smith, Robert D., *Discipline in the Middle School: a Hierarchial Model Keeps Things in Perspective*, Middle School Journal 18 23-5 F 1987.

Steed, David, *Disruptive Pupils, Disruptive Schools: Which is the Chicken? Which is the Egg?* Educational Research 27: 3-8 F 1985.

Sterne, Michael, *Face to Face with Unfairness* (students' right to appeal at Poundswick High School, Manchester, England), The Times Educational Supplement 3617: 4 0 25 1985.

Stressman, C.W., *In-school Suspension: Make it a Place to Grow not just Plant*, The Clearing House 58: 28-31 S 1984.

Sutcliffe, Jeremy, *Suspensions Soar as Deterrent Options Dwindle* (survey on school discipline in Great Britain), The Times Educational Supplement 3755: A5 Je 17 1988.

Symposium, *Teaching Self-discipline, Theory into Practice*, 24: 226-92 Aut 1985.

Symposium, *Reducing Aggressive Behaviour in Schools*, Pointer (Washington, D.C.) 29: 4-54 Wint 1985.

Symposium, *Values and Discipline*, Curriculum Review 26: 14-24+ S/O 1986.

Symposium, *Effectively Disciplined Schools*, NASSP Bulletin 72: 1-6,+ Ja 1988.

Thomas, Jerry R., Lee, Amelia M. and McGee, Lea, *Effects of Individual and Group Contingencies on Disruptive Playground Behavior*, Journal of Research and Development in Education 20: 66-76 Spr 1987.

Thomas, William, *What Makes a Good Discipline Policy?* The Education Digest 54: 40-3 N 1988.

Thomas, William, *To Solve the Discipline Problem: Mix Clear Rules with Consistent Consequences*, The American School Board Journal 175: 30-1 J 1988.

Todd, S., *Improving Our Class*, in 'Students and Teachers: Partners in Classroom Change', edited by J Dunn and H Kirchner, p19-21. Commonwealth Schools Commission, Canberra, Australia, 1987.

Wagner, Jill, *Formulating a Discipline Policy*, NASSP Bulletin 71: 49-50 O 1987.

Wayson, William W. and Lasley, Thomas J., *Climates for Excellence: Schools that Foster Self-discipline*, Phi Delta Kappan 65: 419-21 F 1984.

Wheldall, Kevin and Merrett, Frank, *Which Classroom Behaviours do Primary School Teachers Say They Find Most Troublesome?* Education Review (Albingdon, England) 40 No. 1: 13-27 1988.

Zeidner, Moshe, *The Relative Severity of Common Classroom Management Strategies: the Student's Perspective*, British Journal of Educational Psychology, 58 part 1: 69-77 1988.

Videos

Assertiveness Skills: 1. Persisting; 2. Resisting. Spotlight Training Films, P.O. Box 677, Lane Cove, NSW, Australia, 2066. (1986)

Communication and Counselling Skills. 10 modules: *1. Observation; 2. Attending; 3. Self-awareness; 4. Questioning; 5. Reflection of Content; 6. Reflection of Feeling; 7. Information Giving; 8. Reframing and Interpreting; 9. Confrontation; 10. An Integrative Approach.* Lifeline Queensland, School of Health and Welfare Studies (BCAE), Department of Family and Youth Services, Queensland State Government, Australia. (1988)

Control Theory and Reality Therapy Tapes. Package for schools: *1. Control Theory Lecture; 2. Control Theory and Reality Therapy; 5. Control Theory in the Classroom; 6. Roleplays with Adolescent Clients; 7. Roleplays with Adolescent Clients.* William Glasser, Institute for Reality Therapy, 7301 Medical Centre Drive, Suite 407, Canoga Park, California, U.S.A., 91307. (1988) (818) 888 0688. Australian contact: Judy Hatswell, Australian Guidance and Counselling Association, 37 Oakes Rd., W. Pennant Hills, NSW, 2120. (02) 633 0487.

Every Move You Make, Every Step You Take. Video learning package on discipline steps used in the classroom. Rogers, W.A., Institute of Educational Administration, Geelong, Australia, 1989.

Helping Us, Helping Them. Video exploring issues in classroom discipline. Rogers, W.A., Western Metropolitan Region, Ministry of Education, Melbourne, Australia, 1986.

Listening: The Problem Solver. Callner Film Productions, Jason Films.

Mission Impossible: Managing Groups Effectively. Teamwork Training Services, Augustine Centre, Australia, 1987.

More Bloody Meetings. Sequel to *Meetings, Bloody Meetings.* John Cleese, Video Arts, 1984.

Say What You Want. Melrose Film Productions, 1988.

The Skilled Helper. Training video for Gerard Egan's book *The Skilled Helper*, (3rd. ed.) Wills, G., Mountain Psychological Associates, Mt. Dandenong, Australia, 1988.

Understanding Leadership Package. Includes Monograph, Facilitators Guide, Workshop Modules and Videotapes. Institute of Educational Administration, P.O. Box 280, Geelong, Australia, 3220. (1987).

About the Authors

Margaret Cowin
B.A. (Melb.), B.Ed. (Monash), T.P.T.C. (Toorak), M.A.Ps.S., M.A.C.E., Reg. Psychologist, Reg. Guidance Officer.

Margaret has held a variety of positions in the education field — primary teacher, guidance officer, senior guidance officer, policy analyst with the State Board of Education, senior education officer and now a manager of a School Support Centre. She has also been very involved with schools as a parent of three children.

Liz Freeman
B.A. (Melb.), Dip. Ed. (Melb.), M.Ed. (Monash), M.A.Ps.S., Reg. Psychologist, Reg. Guidance Officer.

Liz originally worked as a secondary teacher and then practised for eleven years as an educational psychologist in the Ministry of Education. She was seconded to the Institute of Educational Administration as a syndicate consultant before leaving the Ministry to take up her current position as Senior Lecturer and Co-ordinator of the Graduate Diploma in Student Welfare at Hawthorn Institute of Education. Liz is interested in the development of positive programs and processes in schools which will enhance the learning and welfare of all students.

Alan Farmer
T.P.T.C. (Toorak), B.Com. (Melb.), B.Ed. (Melb.), M.Ed. (Monash), F.A.Ps.S., Reg. Psychologist, Reg. Guidance Officer.

Alan has worked in primary, secondary, technical and tertiary education. He has been a teacher, psychologist and principal guidance officer with the Ministry of Education. He is the proud father of three children.

Meryl James
B.Sc. (Hons) (Monash), M.Ed. (Monash).

Meryl worked as a psychology officer with the Ministry of Education for seven years, specialising in research and resources for the former Counselling, Guidance and Clinical Services section. Prior to her time as a psychology officer, she completed an M.Ed. at Monash University for which she studied children's perception of emotion in other people. She is the mother of two children.

Ailsa Drent
B.A.(Melb.), M.Ed. (Monash), T.P.T.C. (Toorak), M.A.Ps.S., Reg. Psychologist, Reg. Guidance Officer.

Ailsa has taught at primary, secondary and tertiary levels of education. She initially joined the school guidance service in 1967 and has held a number of positions of responsibility. She is married with four sons and has dovetailed her role as a parent with professional expertise developed in the field.

Ray Arthur
B.A.(Hons.), T.P.T.C., M.A.Ps.S., Reg. Psychologist, Reg. Guidance Officer.

Ray has taught in primary, post-primary, tertiary and special education settings. He has worked as a guidance officer in metropolitan and country areas and is currently manager of a School Support Centre. He is married and has two sons.